W9-ALM-992

KATHY
FRANK

The
Anti-Psychiatry Bibliography
and Resource Guide
second edition, revised & expanded
K. Portland Frank
Press Gang

Canadian Cataloguing in Publication Data

Frank, K. Portland, 1943–
The anti-psychiatry bibliography and resource guide

ISBN 0-88974-008-9 bd.
ISBN 0-88974-006-2 pa.

1. Antipsychiatry – Bibliography.
2. Psychiatry – Bibliography. I. Title.
Z6664.N5F73 1979 016.6168'9 C79-091176-0

Text copyright © 1979 K. Portland Frank and Press Gang Publishers
Illustration copyright © 1979 K. Portland Frank

First printing September 1979

Printed and published in Canada
by the collective of
Press Gang Publishers,
603 Powell Street,
Vancouver, British Columbia,
Canada

NOTE ON THE SECOND EDITION

This book began as a small project back in the summer of 1973 when I set out to compile an anti-psychiatry bibliography for the Vancouver Mental Patients Association's office research files. After it was completed, M.P.A. decided to publish it as part of the Mental Patients Publishing Project which ran through the summer of 1974 on a Canadian federal government Opportunities for Youth grant.

The following year, M.P.A. turned the *Anti-Psychiatry Bibliography and Resource Guide* over to Press Gang, who then continued to distribute it until their copies sold out in late 1976. At that point, Press Gang called me and asked if I would do an updated edition. I was somewhat unprepared at the time, but got started as best I could.

Several people from Press Gang, M.P.A., and other areas of the psychiatry movement offered invaluable advice, suggestions, information, etc. and before long it was obvious I had embarked on a whole new project. That was three years ago.

Beyond the many-fold increase in length, two other major changes have evolved in the new bibliography. First, the material has been organized so as to make a more cohesive political statement reflecting the perspective of the mental patients liberation and other related movements, especially feminism and anti-capitalism/imperialism. The other change is one of format, moving from a strict bibliography towards more of a "catalogue" style.

The main purpose of *The Anti-Psychiatry Bibliography and Resource Guide* is to provide a useful handbook for persons wishing to explore the failings of the present mental health system, how to change and/or abolish it, and what alternatives there are to this system. It is intended as a political tool for fighting psychiatric oppression in its diverse and ever-expanding ramifications.

Psychiatric institutions as they now stand are grossly unsatisfactory in nearly all respects. Yet at times they end up being the only "asylum" for persons freaking out – what alternatives, really, does our society offer? Many groups such as M.P.A. are working toward developing their own alternatives, but this is slow work. There is also resistance from the outside community: uninformed citizens are wary and would often prefer to see "crazies" kept locked up in mental institutions. So until we can materialize our goal of rendering mental hospitals obsolete, we must continue fighting to achieve interim goals that will protect the rights of patients incarcerated in them.

Beyond this activism for mental patients' rights and the development of alternatives to psychiatric treatment, there also lies the urgent struggle against the ever-increasing encroachment of psychiatric ideology and technology on our everyday lives. The sophisticated arsenal of mind-control weapons presently being developed for purposes of social control places us all in grave danger.

There still remains one twilight area that anti-psychiatry literature to date has not fully explored: the question of *genuine* organic mental disease and how best to deal with it. While throwing out the medical model is absolutely necessary for solving most problems of living, there is a small minority of cases where the model still applies: brain tumors, head injuries, toxic states, etc. For example, there is the controversial "Megavitamin Theory"* of Drs. A. Hoffer and H. Osmond which, on the one hand, can be regarded as the ultimate defence of the medical model, but on the other, may have validity as a case where a person's biochemical balance has become upset to the point of drastically altering consciousness.

We should remember that an analysis of mental suffering that excludes all but social and political causes could become just as absurd as the present medical model. After all, anti-psychiatry is a two-fold movement: it actively pushes to abolish the psychiatric system and other oppressive institutions; but it also seeks out new ways to heal people's mental pain. We certainly do need to get rid of psychiatry and its psychiatrists with their so-called tools of healing — their Thorazine, shock machines, lobotomies — torture methods which reap huge profits while destroying the brains they purport to heal. Yet we still need a few alternative *natural* healing tools. The physical side to mental healing is a thorny ambiguous area and one which psychiatry has blatently mystified and abused. I hope that in the future more anti-psychiatry writers will explore and investigate these questions. One possible model for study is China, where most "hard" psychiatric techniques have been outlawed and replaced by more natural holistic ones such as acupuncture and political study.

While forever aspiring to make this new edition as perfect, all-inclusive and definitive as possible, I have become guilty of holding up the presses. And although even in its present form it still feels more like a working paper than a finished product, we all agreed that the time has come to stop adding to it and *just get it out.*

I'm asking all readers for help in planning a third edition. Please write to me c/o Press Gang Publishers, sending your feedback, criticisms, suggestions, etc. I'd like to hear about new books and other literature, as well as old ones I've managed to leave out. Also, information about mental patients liberation/anti-psychiatry groups and their current projects. Your correspondence is always welcome!

*This theory, in its essence, defines "schizophrenia" as a disease in brain function, especially that of perception, which is caused by a biochemical imbalance related to niacin deficiency and/or an extraordinary need for this vitamin in certain individuals. The cure it proposes is massive doses of niacin. For more information, see Hoffer, Abram and Osmond, Humphrey, **How to Live with Schizophrenia**, Secaucus, N.J.: University Books/Lyle Stewart Inc., 1974.

ACKNOWLEDGEMENTS

Like most books, the *Anti-Psychiatry Bibliography* would not have been possible without the contributions of many persons besides the one whose name appears on the cover. I would like to begin by thanking Fran Phillips, who has been my friend and teacher since I first came to M.P.A. and whose collaboration helped produce the section on M.P.A.; also Barry Coull, who provided information and ideas for both the M.P.A. section and the essay on children and psychiatry; Linda Haidei, who also contributed to the M.P.A. section; Jackie Hooper, who provided various information, and in particular an extensive bibliography on patient's rights; Judi Chamberlin for information about the mental patients liberation movement and whose card file bibliography provided many new entries for the 2nd edition; Ted Chabasinski for sending a lot of valuable information and for writing the first draft of the history of the North American Conference on Human Rights and Psychiatric Oppression; Don Weitz, for his letter with constructive suggestions on how I could improve the 2nd edition; Cha and Pat of Seattle for their information on women's spirituality; Wendy Davis for co-counselling references; people at M.P.A. who discussed this project with me and provided information, literature, etc.; workers from the Mental Patients Publishing Project who produced the first edition of the *Bibliography,* namely, Terry Haughian, Barbara Joyce, Eve-Lynne Rubin, and David Wallace; the people who publish the various movement publications from which I drew heavily: *Heavy Daze, Madness Network News, State and Mind, New Women's Survival Sourcebook, and Source Catalog* #3; Press Gang people: Pat Smith for her early suggestions on getting started and help with editing later on; Penny Goldsmith for help editing essays and typesetting; Laurie McGuigan for help with essays; Sarah Davidson for production planning; Billie Carroll and Nancy Pollak who brought everything through to its final concrete form; and finally, I'd like to thank Persimmon Blackbridge who helped write the essays on Psychiatry and Women, and who provided level-headed criticism of all the essays and graphics.

K. Portland Frank,
Vancouver, 1979

CONTENTS

INTRODUCTION: THE ANTI-PSYCHIATRY MOVEMENT AND ITS WRITINGS

Anti-psychiatry is a present day political movement to free mental patients from psychiatric oppression. Its fundamental ideology begins with the rejection of medical and psychiatric definitions of mental illness; its ultimate goal is to smash the enormous power wielded by the mental health system.

Psychiatry is the official institution within our scientific/industrial class society authorized to control and punish all persons unable and/or unwilling to fit into the roles that society demands.

Psychiatry as a branch of modern medicine was largely formulated during the 19th century, its ideology crystalizing in the latter decades as a result of theoretical works published by Emil Kraeplin (who first classified mental diseases) and Sigmund Freud (who invented psychoanalysis). The practice of isolating "mad" persons in special institutions and treating them through objective clinical study was, ironically, a breakthrough from the previous custom of accusing them of demonic possession. In the mid-17th century, Philippe Pinel spoke against the chaining of inmates, and promoted the psychological and medical models of madness. Similarly, Dorothea Dix's protest against conditions in 19th century Massachussetts called for the creation of state mental hospitals with skilled employees. But even as psychiatry and mental institutions evolved, various anti-psychiatry trends were surfacing. In 1873, Elizabeth P. Ware Packard, an outstanding 19th century ex-patient activist, published her monumental critique of institutional psychiatry, *Modern Persecution; or Insane Asylums Unveiled.* Early in the 20th century, ex-patient Clifford Whittingham Beers (author of *A Mind That Found Itself,* 1908) began the Mental Hygiene Movement which was aimed at reforming mental institutions.

The modern day movement had its beginnings around 1960. Some of the pioneering writers were R.D. Laing (*The Divided Self,* 1959), Thomas Szasz (*The Myth of Mental Illness,* 1961), and Erving Goffman (*Asylums,* 1959). Among the hundreds of books and thousands of essays that have come out of the movement, it is impossible to single out the most important work. Laing's *The Politics of Experience and the Bird of Paradise* is perhaps the most famous and, in many ways, best captures the spirit of the anti-psychiatry movement as it first emerged; of the literature from the early 70's, one outstanding landmark is Phyllis Chesler's *Women and Madness* which, using a feminist perspective, explores how psychiatry furthers the oppression of a particular group of people; from the mid 70's, the *Position Paper of the Fourth Annual North American Conference on Human Rights and Psychiatric Oppression* is the key document issued by the psychiatrically oppressed on their own behalf. These three works typify how anti-psychiatry has evolved from a largely theoretical movement dominated by professionals to a political force now under the direction of ex-mental patients.

The term "anti-psychiatry" came into use around 1970 when David Cooper (then an associate of Laing) published his book, *Psychiatry and Anti-Psychiatry*, criticizing the violence of institutional psychiatry and arguing for more freely structured alternatives.

In his essay on the anti-psychiatry movement in 1972, Ruitenbeek (*Going Crazy*, Introduction) identified two main factions: British anti-psychiatry and American Radical Therapy. Since the mid 70's the movement has spread and ramified. The chart in Appendix C (pages 155-157) was prepared to help identify and compare current groups and trends in anti-psychiatry. This chart is intended only as a rough guide; apologies to all those who have suffered some inevitable form of misrepresentation in the process. Also, it includes mainly English-speaking groups although the movement — let it be known — is going strong in such places as France, Germany, Holland, Japan and elsewhere.

I. The Mental Patient
Experience

I THE MENTAL PATIENT EXPERIENCE

a) Autobiographical Accounts

First-hand accounts of what it means to be a mental patient, documented by experts – mental patients and ex-patients. (However, it should be noted – and emphasized – that the label of "mental patient" is itself now being rejected by most Movement people, and has been replaced by a more telling self-definition, i.e. "psychiatric inmate.") This section includes both pure autobiography and autobiographical novels. Included also are some famous "cases" which have been used by writers from Freud to Szasz to support various theories. A wide range of perspectives can be seen in the ways these persons have responded to their experiences of madness and "therapy". Yet although some writers do appear to recommend practices used by their psychiatric jailers, almost every one expresses feelings of being intimidated and oppressed by the institutions that purport to help them. Many other short accounts not included here can be found in various anthologies and journals which constantly publish articles, reports, letters, poems, graphics, etc. submitted by psychiatric inmates and ex-inmates.

Anonymous. "Ordeals in a mental hospital." In *Rough times*, ed. by J. Agel. New York: Ballantine, 1973.

Experience of a woman who spent time in a mental hospital. Describes some of the rip-offs that happened to her and other patients.

Barnes, Mary. "Flection/reflection." In *The radical therapist.* ed. by J. Agel. New York: Ballantine, 1971.

A brief account of the journey through madness taken by Mary Barnes at Kingsley Hall.

Barnes, Mary and Berke, Joseph. *Mary Barnes: two accounts of a journey through madness.* Middlesex: Penguin, 1973.

"I am forty-eight years old. The five years at Kingsley Hall were all my years, for therein was held my past, my present and my future. The nurse, the teacher, fled; the child returned, grew as never before, in body and soul." This is the story of Mary Barnes, Kingsley Hall's most famous resident.

Bateson, Gregory, ed. *Perceval's Narrative: a patient's account of his psychosis, 1830-1832.* Stanford, Ca.: Stanford University Press, 1961.

This important 19th century autobiographical document recounts Perceval's experiences during involuntary committal for three year psychotic episode. Edited with lengthy introduction by Bateson, who uses Perceval's case to lend support to his thesis that the "schizophrenic voyage" is often a journey into self-discovery and eventual healing. This work is quoted and discussed by Laing in *The Politics of Experience* as he leads up to his manifesto that: "Madness need not be all breakdown. It may also be breakthrough. It is potentially liberation and renewal as well as enslavement and existential death."

Beers, Clifford Whittingham. *A mind that found itself: an autobiography.* Garden City, New York: Doubleday, 1953.

Important autobiographical work written by an ex-mental patient who launched the mental hygiene movement of the early 20th century. His recommendations for reform of institutional conditions were based on his own experience and insights gained during an involuntary committal. The present issue is a posthumously revised edition of the 1908 classic, expanded by the American Foundation for Mental Hygiene to include a supplement on the mental hygiene movement.

Bogan, Louise. *What the woman lived: selected letters of Louise Bogan 1920-1970.* Edited by Ruth Limmer. New York: Harcourt Brace Jovanovitch, 1973.

Contains many poetic letters written from the mental institution where Louise Bogan was incarcerated in 1930.

Boisen, Anton T. *Out of the depths.* New York: Harper & Row, 1960.

A second book by the author of *The Exploration of the Inner World* (see II-b, Other Related Social/Phenomenological Studies). This is an account of Boisen's own schizophrenic experiences, which he insists are of "unquestionable religious value."

Bowers, Malcolm B. Jr. *Retreat from sanity: the structure of emerging psychosis.* See II-b, Other Related Social/Phenomenological Studies.

C.B. "Letter." In *The radical therapist,* ed. by J. Agel. New York:Ballantine, 1971.

C.B. spent several years in a mental hospital and is now out. Describes oppressive experiences of "therapy programmes" in mental institutions.

Chamberlin, Judi. "Struggling to be born." In *Women look at psychiatry,* ed. by Dorothy E. Smith and Sara J. David. Vancouver: Press Gang Publishers, 1975.

East coast member/activist of Mental Patients Liberation Front writes about personal experiences with psychiatry. Describes the road that leads women to Rockland State Hospital.

Coate, Morag. *Beyond all reason.* Philadelphia: J.B. Lippincott, 1965.

"Morag Coate has given us one of the best available descriptions of the experience of being mad . . . a picture of what it is to be a schizophrenic *person* rather than an alien and inhuman schizophrenic case." (R.D. Laing, Preface)

Donaldson, Kenneth. *Insanity inside out.* New York: Crane Publishers, 1976.

Documents important legal precedent. Personal experience of incarceration for fifteen years in Florida hellhole which ended with court case and Supreme Court ruling (1975) that persons judged mentally ill but not dangerous have constitutional right to liberty.

Farmer, Frances. *Will there really be a morning?* New York: Dell, 1972.

Autobiography of film star in the 30's who spent eight years in a state hospital.

Frame, Janet. *Faces in the water.* New York: George Braziller, 1961.

Autobiographical account of Frame's experiences in New Zealand mental hospital. It describes the mechanical illogical routines of hospital life.

Glenn, Michael, ed. *Voices from the asylum.* See XI-b, Anthologies.

Greenberg, Joanne. *I never promised you a rose garden.* New York: New American Library/Signet, 1964.

Classic autobiographical novel about Greenberg's own journey into madness when she was a sixteen year old girl. Documents her experiences during the three years she spent in mental hospital and her eventual return to reality.

Gothin, Janet and Gothin, Paul. *Too much anger, too many tears: a personal triumph over psychiatry.* New York: Quadrangle, 1975.

Hirschman, Jack, ed. *Artaud anthology.* San Francisco: City Lights Books, 1965.

Collection of essays by ex-inmate writer, Antonin Artaud. Contains good and powerful critiques of psychiatry.

Jefferson, Lara. *These are my sisters: a journal from the inside of insanity.* Garden City, New York: Anchor Press/Doubleday, 1975.

Posthumously published (1948) journal of a young woman who was diagnosed as "schizophrenic", committed to a midwestern mental institution and died in the 1940's.

Kaplan, Bert, ed. *The inner world of mental illness: a series of first person accounts of what it was like.* See XI-b, Anthologies.

Miller, Nadine. "Letter to her psychiatrist." In *The radical therapist,* ed. by J. Agel. New York: Ballantine, 1971.

Letter by a woman who is turning from oppressive therapy by male psychiatrist to the Women's Movement. She explicitly states her reasons for this change.

Medvedev, Z. and Medvedev, R. *A question of madness*. Translated by Ellen de Kadt. New York: Knopf, 1971.

Mental Patients Publishing Project, eds. *Madness unmasked.* See XI-b, Anthologies.

Moore, Harriet. *From madness to mysticism.* Available from: Artists and Alchemists, 31 Chapel Lane, Riverside, Connecticut, U.S.A.

Graphic journey by artist, documenting her journey through confusion and despair into mystical experiences.

O'brien, Barbara. *Operators and things: the inner life of a schizophrenic.* London: Elek Books, 1960.

". . . a beautifully lucid, autobiographical description of a psychotic episode that lasted six months and whose healing function is clear . . . " (R.D. Laing, *The Politics of Experience*)

Plath, Sylvia. *The bell jar.* New York: Doubleday, 1971.

Plath's autobiographical novel about her experience as a mental patient.

Plath, Sylvia. "Johnny Panic and the Bible of dreams." In *The age of madness,* ed. by T.S. Szasz. Garden City, New York: Anchor Press/Doubleday, 1973.

"Sylvia Plath (1932-63), writer and poet, waged an unsuccessful war against the constraints of the feminine role, was labelled mentally ill, hospitalized, and treated with electroshock. She died by suicide. The following selection is a thinly veiled account of her experiences as a mental-hospital patient." (T.S. Szasz)

Schreber, Daniel Paul. *Memoirs of my nervous illness.* London: William Dawson & Sons, 1955. Trans. and ed., with Introduction and Notes by Ida Macalpine and Richard A. Hunter.

Considered a classic document in psychiatry. Freud used it as the basis for his theory that paranoia is a reaction formation against homosexual feelings. Recently, British anti-psychiatrist Morton Schatzman analyzed these memoirs in terms of the destructive role of family and authoritarian child-rearing practices. See Schatzman, *Soul Murder,* II-a-i, The British Anti-psychiatry School.

Stefan, Gregory. *In search of sanity: the journal of a schizophrenic.* New Hyde Park, New York: University Books, 1965.

Written by a journalist who suddenly cracked up in his early 30's. Presents detailed description of his generally useless encounters with traditional psychiatrists (one of whom wrecked Stefan's marriage as part of his "therapy") and institutions. Stefan says he had always felt that physical sickness was the true cause of his insanity and that when, several years later, he heard about megavitamin therapy and tried it out, it cured him.

Szasz, Thomas S., ed. *The age of madness: the history of involuntary mental hospitalization presented in selected texts.* See XI-b, Anthologies.

Tarsis, Valeriy. *Ward 7: an autobiographical novel.* Trans. by Katya Brown. London: Collins & Havrill Press, 1965.

Autobiographical novel about Russian writer who undergoes experience of involuntary commital to mental hospital in Kruschev's Russia.

Vonnegut, Mark. *The Eden Express: a personal account of schizophrenia.* New York: Praeger, 1975.

As a male member of a social class more privileged than most other writers represented here, Vonnegut's experiences with psychiatric institutions differed accordingly. These experiences led him to embrace the medical model.

Vonnegut, Mark. "Why I want to bite R.D. Laing." *Harpers* 248(1487) (April 1974): 90-2.

Vonnegut says that madness is not what Laing promised it would be.

Wales, Byron G. "Adjustment to the total institution." In *The age of madness,* ed. by T.S. Szasz. Garden City, New York: Anchor Press/Doubleday, 1973.

Wales spent many years of intermittent hospitalization. Describes what happens to people as they become institutionalized and dependent on the mental institution. "Hospitalization may have eradicated the overt symptoms of his illness at the expense of his character, personality, and individuality as a human being."

b) General Fiction

Enlightened tales, past and present, about the mental health business and its reluctant consumers. Some science fiction works with speculative models of mental health care systems for the future.

Breggin, Peter R. *The crazy from the sane.* New York: L.Stuart, 1971.

Novel about a young psychiatrist-in-training who becomes corrupted by the institution he is working in. Includes journey into a state hospital's back ward (where all patients are called "Jack" and it is impossible to tell "the crazy from the sane"). Plot revolved around defeat in involuntary committal case. Breggin's politics in this book are distinctly Szaszian.

Chekhov, Anton P. "Ward No. 6." In *Seven short novels by Chekhov.* New York: Bantam, 1963.

Story of a doctor who eventually becomes classified as insane because of his friendship with a mental patient, and his inability to deal with the "normal" society around him.

Davis, Johanna. *Life signs.* New York: Dell, 1974.

This short novel is an indictment against a psychiatrist and his oppressive treatment of a woman patient.

DeAssis, M. "The psychiatrist." In *The psychiatrist and other stories,* by M. DeAssis. Berkeley: University of California Press, 1963.

Written in 1881-2. Story about involuntary committal which worked against the interests of the person incarcerated.

Dick, Philip K. *Clans of the alphane moon.* New York: Ace, 1964.

Science fiction novel about society of madpersons. This and many of Dick's other books deal with alternative roles for mental patients in hypothetical societies.

Dunne, John Gregory. *Vegas, a memoir of a dark season.* New York: Warner Books, 1975.

Novel presenting difficulties encountered by person having a mental breakdown.

Gibson-Gilford, Margaret. *The butterfly ward.* Toronto: Oberon, 1976.

An excellent collection of short stories which describes women coping with the vagrancies of the system both inside and outside of mental institutions.

Kesey, Ken. *One flew over the cuckoo's nest.* New York: New American Library/Signet, 1963.

A misogynist analysis of the injustices of a mental institution, this novel makes a bold and colourful attempt to obscure the true causes of psychiatric oppression. The good insights it actually does provide about life in institutions tend, in every way, to get dragged under by the story's ubiquitous sexist mentality.

Delany, Samuel R. *Dhalgren.* New York: Bantam, 1975.

Science fiction novel about madness and a mad world. An unusual male writer, Delany is actually willing to deal with sexism in his books, and has used some novels to put forth models for non-sexist societies.

LeGuin, Ursula. *The lathe of heaven.* New York: Avon, 1973.

Science fiction novel by feminist writer about dreams and a psychiatrist who plans to take over the world but fails.

Lessing, Doris. *The four-gated city.* New York: Bantam, 1970.

"A visionary novel about the role of 'insane' people in the transformation of society." (Mad Librarian)

Piercy, Marge. *Woman on the edge of time.* New York: Alfred A. Knopf, 1976.

This feminist science fiction novel really captures the mental patient experience. It is about a Chicana woman who is victimized by racism, sexism, imperialism, and later a state mental hospital ward. Her story is counterpointed by a totally different world of the future.

Ward, Mary Jane. *The snake pit.* New York: New American Library/Signet, 1946.

A classic, this novel unveils the horrors of madness and life inside a state mental hospital as seen through the eyes of a woman inmate.

c) Other Misc. Literature

Alvarez, A. *The savage god: a study of suicide.* New York: Bantam, 1973.

In depth study of suicide in our time. Includes account of the last days of Sylvia Plath. Helps explain why many creative people choose death. Examines history, myths, literature, psychology, and technology of self-destruction.

Milford, Nancy. *Zelda.* New York:Avon, 1974.

Biography about famous woman patient, Zelda Fitzgerald. Zelda's life is also discussed by Chesler in *Women and Madness* (see VII-a, Women: General Works).

Reed, David. *Anna.* See II-a-ii, British School Criticisms and Reviews.

Special Issue: Women and mental health. *Chomo-Uri* 3(2) Fall/Winter 1976.

Collection of women's poems, prose, graphics. Material describes women in various stages/aspects of madness and mental health. Much of it expresses despair encountered within mental institutions and therapy. Back issues available for $1.00 each from: Chomo-Uri, 506 Goodell Hall, University of Massachussets, Amherst, Mass. 01003, U.S.A.

II. The Politics
Mary Barnes
of Sanity
and Madness

II THE POLITICS OF SANITY AND MADNESS

This section consists of studies and theories in the sociology and phenomenology of "mental illness" that are generally associated with the formulations of R.D. Laing and British anti-psychiatry.

a) The British Anti-Psychiatry School

The oldest school, British anti-psychiatry has been built around the writings of Laing and Cooper. The school began with a focus on the role of family structure in the development of mental illness, but as time went by, it turned its attention to a general indictment of oppressive social structure. Some of its studies approached sanity and madness within a dialectical framework. The British school also made explorations into the existential and mystical significance of the "psychotic breakdown". In addition to a large volume of theoretical works, this school produced some important early experiments in anti-psychiatry, the most famous of which was Kingsley Hall, an alternative treatment program sponsored by the Philadelphia Association and R.D. Laing, its chairman. David Cooper's Villa-21 was another, yet earlier, anti-psychiatry experiment. While advancing radical views on the nature of mental illness and the dubiousness of conventional treatment, the British School has always continued to support psychotherapy directed by psychiatrists.

British anti-psychiatry is important to the present-day anti-psychiatry/mental patients liberation movement because it opened up several directions of varying revolutionary potential during the 1960's. Sadly, however, their writings of the 1970's have abandoned many of their own earlier insights and have, instead, degenerated into non-political directions — mystical, poetic, psychoanalytical, etc. Today, several of their households for mental patients continue to operate around London under the auspices of the Philadelphia and Arbours Associations.

i) Writings and Interviews

Barnes, Mary and Berke, Joseph. *Mary Barnes: two accounts of a journey through madness.* See I-a, Autobiographical Accounts.

Berke, Joseph, ed. *Counter-culture: the creation of an alternative society.* See XI-b, Anthologies.

Cooper, David. "Beyond words." In *To free a nation: the dialectics of liberation,* ed. by David Cooper. Middlesex: Penguin, 1968.

Cooper, David, ed. *To free a nation: the dialectics of liberation.* Middlesex: Penguin, 1968.

Contains some of the principle addresses delivered at The Congress on the Dialectics of Liberation, London, July 1967. This Congress was organized by four psychiatrists prominent in the British anti-psychiatry movement: R.D. Laing, David Cooper, Joseph Berke, and Leon Redler. For details, see XI-b, Anthologies.

Cooper, David. *Psychiatry and anti-psychiatry.* London: Granada/Paladin, 1970.

"What I have attempted . . . is to take a look at the person who has been labelled schizophrenic in his actual human context and to inquire how this label came to be attached to him, by whom it was attached, and what it signifies for both the labellers and the labelled." Also attacks the question of violence in psychiatry. Later chapters outline principles of an experimental unit for young patients within a large mental hospital, and gives an account of Cooper's experiment, Villa-21.

Cooper, David. *The death of the family.* New York: Random House/Vintage, 1971.

"Taking off from the work with Laing and Esterson on families and schizophrenia, he has extended the critique – in a revolutionary world view – to the nuclear family in general . . . a real fusion of Anti-Psychiatry with radical-revolutionary politics....The movement Cooper sees is for the gradual freeing up of one-to-one relationships, the demise of the nuclear family and its being replaced by new communes and collectives in which relationships could develop unilaterally....Presents us with a model for social change, carried out in small-living-collectives." (Michael Glenn, Review, *Rough Times* 2(4))

Cooper, David. *The grammar of living: an examination of political acts.* London: Penguin/Allen Lane, 1974.

A grammar for the expansion of human activities beyond their usual restrictive confines.

Cooper, David. *The language of madness.* Middlesex: Penguin, 1978.

Esterson, Aaron. *The leaves of spring: a study in the dialectics of madness.* Middlesex: Penguin, 1970.

"Esterson has done two things: First, he has taken the family of Sarah Danzig (from *Sanity, Madness, and the Family*) and greatly expanded it, explaining nearly all of the behaviour of the family members in the light of real circumstances. Second, he has written . . . about the theory and methodology of dialectical materialism as applied to psychology." (Phil Brown, Review, *Rough Times* 3(5))

Interview with David Cooper. In *Going crazy: the radical therapy of R.D. Laing and others,* ed. by H.M. Ruitenbeek. New York: Bantam, 1972.

This brief interview first appeared in the *London International Times.* Cooper discusses the rationale behind establishing "liberated zones in London" (e.g. restaurants) where people can meet and dissolve binary roles so as to take leadership into their own hands.

Laing, R.D. "Series and nexus in the family." *New Left Review* I5 (1963): 7-14.

Laing, R.D. *The divided self: an existential study in sanity and madness.* Middlesex: Penguin, 1965.

Laing's first important work: "A study of schizoid and schizophrenic persons; its basic purpose is to make madness, and the process of going mad, comprehensible . . . further . . . to give in plain English an account, in *existential* terms, of some forms of madness."

Laing, R.D. "Mystification, confusion and conflict." In *Intensive family therapy,* ed. by I. Boszormenyi and J.L. Framo. New York: Harper & Row, 1965.

Laing, R.D. "Family and individual structure." In *The predicament of the family,* ed. by P. Lomas. London: Hogarth Press, 1967.

Laing, R.D. *The politics of experience and the bird of paradise.* Middlesex: Penguin, 1967.

The Bible of Laingian anti-psychiatry. A compilation of essays derived from some of Laing's lectures and essays between 1962 and 1965. "No one can begin to think, feel or act now except from the starting-point of his or her own alienation. We shall examine some of its forms in the following pages . . . Alienation as our present destiny is achieved only by the outrageous violence perpetuated by human beings on human beings."

Laing, R.D. "The study of family and social contexts in relation to the origin of schizophrenia." In *The origins of schizophrenia,* ed. by J. Romano. Proceedings of the first Rochester International Conference on Schizophrenia. March 29-31, 1976. New York: Excerpta Medica Foundation, 1967.

Laing criticizes this psychiatric Congress, in which he participated, for trying to determine the origin of something (i.e. schizophrenia) they can't even properly define. Also discusses Kingsley Hall, and suggests that the term "schizophrenia" be replaced by "metanoia", meaning "change of mind" or "conversion". Concludes that "the concept of schizophrenia is a kind of conceptual straightjacket that severely restricts the possibilities of both psychiatrists and patients."

Laing, R.D. "The obvious." In *To free a nation: the dialectics of liberation,* ed. by David Cooper. Middlesex: Penguin, 1968. (Also included in H.M. Ruitenbeck, *Going Crazy.*)

A statement of Laing's political views.

Laing, R.D. *Self and others.* 2nd ed. Middlesex: Penguin, 1972.

"I shall try to depict persons within a social system or 'nexus' of persons, in order to try to understand some of the ways in which each affects each person's experience of himself and of how interaction takes form. Each contributes to the other's fulfilment or destruction."

Laing, R.D. *Knots.* Middlesex: Penguin, 1971.

Written in the form of brief poems, dialogues, and diagrams. "The patterns delineated here have not yet been classified by a Linnaeus of human bondage . . . . Words that come to mind to name them are: knots, tangles, frankles, *impasses*, disjunctions, whirligogs, binds."

Laing, R.D. "Metanoia: some experiences at Kingsley Hall, London." In *Going crazy: the radical therapy of R.D. Laing and others,* ed. by H.M. Ruitenbeek. New York: Bantam, 1972.

Laing, R.D. *The politics of the family and other essays.* New York: Random House/Vintage, 1972.

The Politics of the Family consists of five essays taken from Laing's talks for the Canadian Broadcasting Corporation in its Eighth Series of the Massey Lectures. In them, he sketches tentative outlines for a systematic calculus of interpersonal relationships. He extends his previous concepts of family to include several generations, all of whom partake in perpetuating the family drama or pageant. The majority of this work is devoted to examining the discontinuity between behaviour and experience, along with the mystifying role of rules and metarules in perpetuating this discontinuity.
Also includes: "The Family and the 'Family' " (revised from "Individual and Family Structure" in *The Predicament of the Family*, ed. by P. Lomas. London: Hogarth Press, 1967); "Intervention in Social Situations" (lecture given at Association of Family Caseworkers, May 1968); "The Study of Family and Social Contexts in Relation to 'Schizophrenia' " (presentation given at APA's 1967 symposium on "The Origins of Schizophrenia").

Laing, R.D. *The facts of life: an essay in feelings, facts, and fantasy.* New York: Pantheon Books, 1975.

"The main fact of life for me is love or its absence." This book is a collection of Laing's thoughts about the life cycle of a human being. It contains prescriptions for the adult birth sequence. Text is spiked with tidbits of gossip about Laing's own past.

Laing, R.D. *Do you love me? An entertainment in conversation and verse.* New York: Pantheon Books, 1976.

" . . . resembles *Knots*, but goes further, both in its form and in its subject matter. Dr. Laing ranges across the span of human emotions, from those of families and lovers to those of strangers and enemies. His verses include brief *apercus*, complex exchanges, new lyrics for old songs, and savage maxims for everyday life." (from jacket review)

Laing, R.D. and Cooper, David. *Reason and violence: a decade of Sartre's philosophy 1950-1960.* New York: Random House/Pantheon, 1971.

A condensation of Sartre's work to about one-tenth of its original scale. Difficult to read. Discusses developments in Sartre's thought since *Being and Nothingness,* particularly *Critique of Dialectical Reason.* Shows Sartre's work as leading further toward a social interaction theory; some of Sartre's social concepts, like "process and praxis", were used in Laing's research for *Sanity, Madness, and the Family.*

Laing, R.D. and Esterson, A. "The collusive function of pairing in analytic groups." *British Journal of Medical Psychology* 31(1958) 117-23.

Laing, R.D. and Esterson, A. *Sanity, madness, and the family: families of schizophrenics*. Middlesex: Penguin, 1970.

Presents case histories and dialogues from taped interviews of 11 women diagnosed as schizophrenic and their families. This record was made over a five year period dating from 1958. Central thesis is that "[in] this book, we believe that we show that the experience and behaviour of schizophrenics is much more socially intelligible than has come to be supposed by most psychiatrists."

Laing, R.D., Phillipson, H. and Lee, A.R. *Interpersonal perception: a theory and a method of research*. London: Tavistock, 1966.

"The central theme of this book is the experiences, perceptions, and actions which occur when two human beings are engaged in a meaningful encounter . . . the method . . . comes to terms with the way in which one person's position is experienced by the other, so that the first may become aware of how he looks in the eyes of the other . . . . Most of the material in this monograph is elaborated around the relations of husband and wife; but the application of the method clearly extends to all other dyads." (Marie Jahoda, Foreward)

Laing, R.D., Phillipson, H. and Lee, A.R. "The spiral of perspectives." *New Society* (November 10, 1966): 713-16.

Rossabi, Andrew. "Anti-psychiatry: an interview with Dr. Joseph Berke." In *R.D. Laing and anti-psychiatry*, ed. by R. Boyers and R. Orrill. New York: Harper & Row, 1971. (Also included in H.M. Ruitenbeek, *Going Crazy*.)

About Berke, his association with Laing, Mary Barnes, and Kingsley Hall. Also discusses definitions of "insanity" and the rationale of mental institutions. Berke was Mary Barne's therapist and co-author of *Mary Barnes: Two Accounts of a Journey Through Madness.*

Rossabi, Andrew. "On paranoia: an interview with Morton Schatzman." *Issues in Radical Therapy* (1973), *1*(3).

Discusses the Arbours Housing Association, definitions and causes of "mental illness", especially "paranoia". Schatzman also talks about the Schreber case and Schreber's father's child-rearing practices to illustrate how "paranoia" and delusions get started.

Schatzman, Morton. "Madness and morals." In *Counter culture: the creation of an alternative society*, ed. by J. Berke. London: Peter Owen/Fire Books, 1969. (Also included in R. Boyers and R. Orrill, *R.D. Laing and Anti-Psychiatry*.)

Schatzman, Morton. *Soul murder: persecution in the family.* New York: New American Library/Signet, 1974.

" . . . examines the 'mental illness' of Daniel Paul Schreber, whose Memoirs are considered a classic . . . and contrasts them with the work of Schreber's father, Daniel Gottlieb Moritz Schreber . . . a noted authority on child-rearing . . . . We are shown how all the 'symptoms' of young Schreber's 'illness' are directly attributable to his father's authoritarian theory and practice of child-rearing . . . speaks of the destructive role of the family in terms which will be familiar to readers of Laing, Cooper, and Esterson . . . " (Phil Brown, Review, *Rough Times*, Vol. 3, No. 5)

ii) Outside Criticisms and Reviews

"An R.D. Laing Symposium with R. Coles, L. Farber, E. Friedenberg, K. Lux." In *R.D. Laing and anti-psychiatry*, ed. by R. Boyers and R. Orrill. New York: Harper & Row, 1971.

A group of psychiatrists theorize about Laing's work.

Boyers, Robert and Orrill, Robert, eds. *R.D. Laing and anti-psychiatry.* See XI-b, Anthologies.

Brown, Phil. "R.D. Laing's fantastic voyage." *State and Mind* 5(6) (June-July 1977): 43-4.

A non-flattering review of Laing's book, *The Facts of Life.* In it, Brown outlines British Anti-Psychiatry's downhill journey since the early 1970's: "From the insightful analysis of family and schizophrenia, David Cooper moved to preaching adventuristic slogans of 'smash the bourgeois nuclear family'. From the attempt at a Marxist exploration of the social origins of mental illness, Laing went on to thoroughly mystical speculation on intrauterine life. From dialectical studies of class and family connections, Esterson retreated to a dogmatic psychoanalytic focus on anality." Brown suggests that this outcome can be traced, in part, to the British School's underlying currents of idealism which allowed certain things to be analyzed outside of the context of their social origins. Another drawback was their isolation from political activism, while at the same time focusing a lot of energy on "the poetic nuances" decorating their statements. In conclusion, he writes: "*The Facts of Life*, coming on the heels of *Knots,* signals the probable end of R.D. Laing's productive life."

Brown, Phil. "Review: Recent anti-psychiatry books." *Rough Times* (1973), *3*(5): 19.

Descriptions plus comparison of Schatzman's *Soul Murder* and Esterson's *The Leaves of Spring*, which are "very important books in understanding the latest developments in anti-psychiatry and in gaining much insight into the maddening role of the family." Says that Esterson's book goes beyond Schatzman's because it offers dialectical framework.

Brown, Phil. *Towards a Marxist psychology.* New York: Harper and Row, 1974.

Discusses the relationship between class structure, capitalism, and the mental health industry. Includes criticisms of Laing and other theorists.

Chesler, Phyllis. Chapter 3: The clinicians. In *Women and madness*. New York: Avon, 1973.

Criticizes Laing and Esterson (*Sanity, Madness, and the Family*), Cooper (*The Death of the Family*), Szasz, and other theorists from feminist perspective. Chesler believes that none of them have gone far enough in understanding the problems and situation unique to women in sex roles.

Evans, Richard I. *R.D. Laing: the man and his ideas*. New York: E.P. Dutton, 1976.

Dialogue between Laing and Evans covers wide range of topics: Freud, Bateson, schizophrenia, mysticism, therapy, Laing's position as a celebrity. Includes biographical essay by Peter Mezan, and a hitherto unpublished study by Laing of Kallman and Slater's genetic theory of schizophrenia.

Friedenberg, Edgar Z. *R.D. Laing*. New York: Viking Press, 1974.

An analysis of Laing's writings and philosophy. Discusses the philosophical implications of Laing's ideas.

Gordon, James S. "Who is mad? Who is sane? R.D. Laing in search of a new psychiatry." In *Going crazy: the radical therapy of R.D. Laing and others*, ed. by H.M. Ruitenbeek. New York: Bantam, 1972.

An early biographical account of Laing's psychiatric pilgrimage. Written by one of his admirers (an American psychiatrist) who ventured into London to visit Laing and Kingsley Hall.

Gordon, Jan B. "The meta-journey of R.D. Laing." In *R.D. Laing and anti-psychiatry*, ed. by R. Boyers and R. Orrill. New York: Harper & Row, 1971.

Discusses Laing as explorer engaged in a new mode of mapping the frontiers of consciousness.

Holbrook, David. "R.D. Laing and the death circuit." *Encounter* (1968), *31*: 35-45.

Speculates that Laing's inward journey of *The Bird of Paradise* reflects a schizoid episode in his own career of involvement with schizophrenic patients.

Holbrook, David. "Madness to blame society?" *Twentieth Century* (1969), *177*(1041): 29-36.

Criticism of Laing. Points to dangers of blaming "society" for everything.

Johnston, Jill. "R.D. Laing: the misteek of sighcosis." In *Gullibles Travels.* New York: Link Books, 1974.

Discusses Johnston's own and other public reactions to Laing, Kingsley Hall, and the *Politics of Experience* trip. Includes description of a visit she made to see Laing; points out Laing's lack of feminist consciousness at the time.

Martin, David. "R.D. Laing: psychiatry and apocalypse." In *Going crazy: the radical therapy of R.D. Laing and others*, ed. by H.M. Ruitenbeek. New York: Bantam, 1972.

Criticism of Laing's politics. Identifies Laing as a "romantic anarchist" of the contemporary left. Says that while Laing deplores the present social structure, he fails to offer any systematic alternate program.

Mezan, Peter. "After Freud and Jung, now comes R.D. Laing." *Esquire* 77(1)(January 1972): 92-7, 160-78.

Critical review of Laing.

Mitchell, Juliet. *Psychoanalysis and feminism: Freud, Reich, Laing, and women.* New York: Random House/Vintage, 1975.

Mitchell believes that Freud has ultimately more to offer women's liberation than Reich or Laing.

Nelson, Benjamin. "Afterword: a medium with a message: R.D. Laing." In *R.D. Laing and anti-psychiatry*, ed. by R. Boyers and R. Orrill. New York: Harper & Row, 1971.

Speculates on reasons for the current popularity of Laing's "message", but goes on to say that Laing doesn't have the solution to the problem he has pinpointed.

Nuttall, Jeff. *Bomb culture.* London: MacGibbon and Kee, 1968.

Discusses Laing, Berke, Kingsley Hall, the Free U Movement, and other counter-culture activities of the 1960's; includes discussion of Laing's association with "Sigma", a London-based avant-garde precursor of the counter-cultural Underground.

Orrill, Robert and Boyers, Robert. "Schizophrenia, R.D. Laing, and the contemporary treatment of psychosis: an interview with Dr. Theodore Lidz." In *R.D. Laing and anti-psychiatry*, ed. by R. Boyers and R. Orrill. New York: Harper & Row, 1971.

Lidz, a contemporary "authority", concludes that Laing, the man who wrote "If I could turn you on, if I could drive you out of your wretched mind, if I could tell you I would let you know." is "in such a despairing state that he shouldn't do therapy."

Rapaille, G. *Laing*. Paris: Editions Universitaires, 1972.

A French book dedicated to Laing's work. Laing is known in France as "the pope of anti-psychiatry".

Reed, David. *Anna*. New York: Basic Books, 1976.

A true story about David Reed's wife, who underwent Laingian therapy and later committed suicide. Raises some very important questions.

"Religious Sensibility." *The Listener* (April 23, 1970): 536-7.

Discusses Laing's participation in a BBC radio broadcast on "Religious Sensibility" (Spring 1970). In this broadcast, Laing opposed the rationalist and Marxist view that religion is a reflection of social conditions: "Spiritual sensibility derives its forms, but not its substance, from the forms of society."

Ruitenbeek, Hendrik M., ed. *Going crazy: the radical therapy of R.D. Laing and others*. See XI-b, Anthologies.

Schickel, Richard. "The truth which dares not speak its name." *Harper's Magazine* 242(1451)(April 1971): 104.

Critical review of David Cooper's *The Death of the Family.*

Sedgwick, Peter. "Laing's clangs." *New Society* (January 14, 1970): 103-4.

Discusses pitfalls of Laing's blanket condemnation of society.

Sedgwick, Peter. "R.D. Laing: self, symptom and society." In *R.D. Laing and anti-psychiatry*, ed. by R. Boyers and R. Orrill. New York: Harper & Row, 1971.

Sedgwick is a major Laing scholar. This 50-page essay surveys Laing's intellectual history from the existential origins of *The Divided Self* through to the modified algebra of sets underlying *Knots*. Sedgwick divides Laing's writings into four distinct phases: existential, social, mystical and algebraic. Quite critical in parts, especially about Laing's mystical phase of *The Politics of Experience*.

Siegler, Miriam, Osmond, Humphrey and Mann, Harriet. "Laing's model of madness". In *R.D. Laing and anti-psychiatry*, ed. by R. Boyers and R. Orrill. New York: Harper & Row, 1971.

This group of psychiatric researchers devised a system for classifying models of madness. Their essay attempts to analyse Laing's models from *The Politics of Experience*. They identify three models: Psychoanalytic, Conspirational, and Psychedelic. Laing's Psychedelic model is sharply criticized as misleading.

Sigal, Clancey. *Zone of the interior.* New York: Popular Library, 1978.

A fictionalized account of life with R.D. Laing and the British "masters" during their heyday in the 1960's. Takes a sober look at Kingsley Hall in retrospect, exposing various rip-offs that occurred.

Tyson, A. "Homage to catatonia." *New York Review of Books* 11 (February 1971): 3-6.

Informed critic says Laing withdrew his preface in recent issue of *The Divided Self*, and that this may indicate some "theoretical or ideological backtracking."

Vonnegut, Mark. "Why I want to bite R.D. Laing." See I-a, Autobiographical Accounts.

b) Other Related Social/Phenomenological Studies and Models of Madness.

Bateson, Gregory. *Steps to an ecology of mind*. New York: Ballantine, 1972.

Compilation of Bateson's major essays and lectures, which were spread over 35 years. A book about how ideas interact. "Part III: Form and Pathology in Relationship" contains five essays related to schizophrenia and the double-bind theory.

Bateson G., Jackson, D.D., Haley, J. and Weakland, J. "Towards a theory of schizophrenia." *Behavioural Science* 1(1956): 251-64.

Classic research paper with original presentation of 'double-bind hypothesis" (i.e. that persons are often driven insane by contradictory double messages given by authorities such as families). Much of Laing's work on mystification in families is based on this theory.

Boisen, Anton T. *The exploration of the inner world: a study of mental disorder and religious experience.* New York: Harper & Brothers, 1952.

A classic in its field. Written in 1936 by a minister who suffered a severe breakdown early in his career. Based on his own experiences of hospitalization plus later research on groups of mental patients. Proposes that madness is essentially a spiritual experience in which the individual attempts to reconstruct his world-view following some major catastrophe having undermined his previous beliefs. Both Laing and Silverman models of madness derive from this viewpoint in many essentials.

Boisen, Anton T. *Out of the depths.* See I-a, Autobiographical Accounts.

Boisen, Anton T. "The genesis and significance of mystical identification in cases of mental disorder." *Psychiatry* 15(1952): 287-96.

Bowers, Malcolm B. Jr. *Retreat from sanity: the structure of emerging psychosis*. Baltimore: Penguin, 1974.

A presentation of ". . . patient accounts . . . to illustrate the experiential structure of psychotic consciousness." Personal documents are accompanied by commentaries. Includes discussion of autobiographical madness classics and studies in altered states of consciousness.

Bowers, M. and Freedman, D. " 'Psychedelic' experiences in the acute psychoses." In *Altered states of consciousness*, ed. by Charles T. Tart. New York: Doubleday/Anchor, 1969. (Originally published : *Arch. Gen. Psych.* 15(1966): 240-8).

Cited by Laing as one of three most important documents supporting his postulate that "madness need not be all breakdown . . . " This paper presents scientific evidence that whether a so-called "psychotic experience" is perceived as good or bad depends largely on the cultural context surrounding it.

Braginsky, B.M., Braginsky, D.D. and Ring, K. *Methods of madness: the mental hospital as a last resort*. New York: Holt, Rinehart & Winston, 1969.

Report on a series of studies undertaken by a group of social psychologists on patients in a state mental hospital. Shows that psychiatric paradigm of schizophrenia is inappropriate and that new (social) paradigm is called for. Concludes that "chronic" mental patients are not really crazy but are, in fact, very resourceful individuals who employ a number of active manipulations to keep themselves in hospital as part of a rational strategy undertaken in face of failure to cope successfully with an oppressive society. This book suggests that mental hospitals be replaced by co-operative retreats where such victims can go as required and not be further oppressed by "therapy".

Braginsky, B.M. and Braginsky, D.D. *Mainstream psychology*. New York: Holt, Rinehart & Winston, 1974.

Braginsky, B.M. and Braginsky, D.D. *Hansels and Gretals: studies of children in institutions*. New York: Holt, Rinehart & Winston, 1971.

Dabrowski, Kazimerez. *Positive disintegration*. Ed. with Introduction by Jason Aronson. Boston: Little, Brown & Co., 1964.

Compilation of essays by Polish psychiatrist. An important foundation for Silverman's research into the healing function of mental breakdown: ". . . some of the most profound schizophrenic disorganizations are preludes to impressive reorganization and personality growth – not so much breakdown as breakthrough." (Julian Silverman, "When Schizophrenia Helps," *q.v.* this section). Joseph Berke also refers to Dabrowski's theories in connection with Mary Barnes.

Fischer, Roland. "On creative, psychotic and ecstatic states." In *The highest state of consciousness*, ed. by John White. Garden City, New York: Doubleday/Anchor, 1972.

Outlines a continuous physiological model of arousal that relates schizophrenic states of consciousness to normality, creativity, and mystical ecstasy.

Goffman, Erving. *Asylums: essays on the social situation of mental patients and other inmates*. See IV-a, Mental Hospitals.

Goffman, Erving. *Stigma: notes on the management of spoiled identity.* Englewood Cliffs, N.J.: Prentice-Hall, 1963.

Explores the situation of persons who are disqualified from full social acceptance – the physically deformed, the ex-mental patient, the drug addict, the prostitute, the just plain ugly. Examines alternatives facing such persons. Analyzes the stigmatized individual's feelings about himself and his relationship to "normals", and explains strategies employed in dealing with the refusal of others to accept him.

Haley, J. "The family of the schizophrenic: a model system." *Journal of Nervous and Mental Diseases* 129(1959): 357-74.

Discusses topics similar to those in Laing's *The Politics of the Family.* Analyzes family rules and meta-rules in the mystification process. Haley is a double-bind theorist.

Haley, J. "The art of being schizophrenic." *Voices* 1(1965): 133-47.

Lemert, E. "Paranoia and the dynamics of exclusion." *Sociometry* 25(1962): 2-20.

Lemert says that when people ex-communicate others they develop and perpetuate false beliefs about them. He feels that this process plays an important part in the social life of human groups.

MacNab, Francis A. *Estrangement and relationship: experience with schizophrenics*. New York: Dell, 1965.

". . . this work attempts to bring the insights of psychotherapy, theology and existentialism to the problem of schizophrenia." First half of book is a record of two therapy group meetings conducted with author over fifteen month period; second part is theoretical discussion. R.D. Laing, in his Foreword writes: "I believe this book to be unique, in that it is the most ambitious, and the most successful, attempt by a theologian to bridge the gulf between theology and clinical psychiatry."

Scheff, Thomas J. *Being mentally ill: a sociological theory*. Chicago: Aldine Press, 1966.

Scheff, Thomas J., ed. *Mental illness and social processes.* See XI-b, Anthologies.

Scheff, Thomas J., ed. *Labeling madness.* See XI-b, Anthologies.

Silverman, Julian. "Shamans and acute schizophrenia." *American Anthropologist* 65 (February 1967): 21-31.

Cited by R.D. Laing as another of the three most important documents in support of his statement that "madness need not be all breakdown . . ." Compares systematically the behaviour and experience of persons having "acute schizophrenic breakdowns" with that of inspirational medicine men in primitive cultures. Concludes that these two experiences are essentially the same and that whether they become beneficial or destructive depends mainly on the degree of cultural acceptance accorded them.

Silverman, Julian. "When schizophrenia helps." *Psychology Today* 4(4) (1970): 63-65.

A somewhat less technical discussion of theory presented in "Shamans and Acute Schizophrenia" with report of further research Silverman and associates have been doing in this area at Agnews State Hospital, San Jose, California. Says that when a person is in crisis, resultant psychosis may be simply a unique type of creative response employed by the mind to work through a different type of solution. Also discussion of the contributions of Boisen and Dabrowski (*q.q.v.* in this section) to his theory.

Wapnick, K. "Mysticism and schizophrenia." In *The highest state of consciousness*, ed. by J. White. Garden City, New York: Doubleday/Anchor, 1972.

Compares the mystical and insane experiences, examining some classical religious literature (e.g. St. Theresa, Underhill, William James) and classics in the field of madness (e.g. Freud, Jung, Laing, Morag Coate, John Perceval, Bert Kaplan). Concludes that: "The mystic provides the example of the method whereby the inner and the outer may be joined; the schizophrenic, the tragic result when they are separated."

III. Psychiatry and
the Law

III PSYCHIATRY AND THE LAW

Writings that examine the status of mental patients in western society — from the early origins of lunatic asylums up to and including the present day. This section covers writings related to "mental illness" as a political and legal classification: its history, rationale and ideology. These writings examine how mental patients and mental illness, as well as psychiatrists and psychiatry, came to occupy their current positions in society. Implicit in most of them, and explicit in some (especially III-d, Patients Rights) are ideas on how to change things.

The central idea in this section involves discussion of how the medical model came to be applied to "problems in living" and why this model should be discarded. The leading pioneer theorist in this area is Thomas S. Szasz, and most of the writings listed here are relevant to ideas generally associated with him, including both his own sources and his "students' " works.

a) History of "Mental Illness"

Some basic texts outlining the rise of psychiatry and mental hospitals; many of these works are the background to Szasz's theories of psychiatric persecution. These histories also provide good background for radical feminist analysis. Included also are a few histories of mental healing. Historical analysis continues, as well, in parts (b) and (c) of this section.

Bromberg, Walter. *From shaman to psychotherapist: a history of the treatment of mental illness*. Chicago: Henry Regnery, 1975.

A psychiatrist traces beliefs, attitudes, and techniques of mental healing from primitive magical world views, through the middle ages, and up to the present. Deals mostly with the last 200 years. Some healers he discusses are: Pinnel, Mary Baker Eddy, Freud, Horney, Reich, Berne, Perls, and Laing.

Ehrenreich, Barbara and English, Deirdre. *Complaints and disorders: the sexual politics of sickness*. See VII-a Women:General Works.

Ehrenreich, Barbara and English, Deirdre. *Witches, midwives, and nurses: a history of women healers.* See VII-d, Feminist Therapy.

Foucault, Michel. *Madness and civilization: a history of insanity in age of madness.* Trans. by Richard Howard. New York: Random House, 1965.

A work often quoted by Szasz. Points out how madpersons came to occupy the position of social scapegoat which had been formerly assigned to lepers before the decline of leprosy. Gives portrait of prototypes of mental hospitals (such as "Ships of Fools").

Foucault, Michel. *Birth of the clinic: an archeology of medical perception.* New York: Random House/Vintage, 1974.

Foucault, Michel. *Mental illness and psychology.* Trans. by Alan Sheridan. New York: Harper and Row/Harper Colophon, 1976.

This small treatise examines the strange status of madness.

Neaman, Judith S. *Suggestions of the devil: the origins of madness.* Garden City, New York: Doubleday/Anchor, 1975.

Explains how our attitudes toward the insane are really a carryover from the medieval world; shows how even the terminology used to describe madness has changed very little, and how treatment is approached in much the same way.

Packard, Elizabeth P. *Modern persecution: or, insane asylums unveiled, as demonstrated by the Report of the Investigating Committee of the Legislature of Illinois.* See IV-a. Psychiatry and Institutions: Mental Hospitals.

Packard, Elizabeth P. *Great disclosure of spiritual wickedness in high places: with appeal to the government to protect the inalienable rights of women.* See IV-a, Psychiatry and Institutions: Mental Hospitals.

Rosen, George. *Madness in society*. New York: Harper & Row, 1967.

Rosen, G. "Social attitudes to irrationality and madness in 17th and 18th century Europe." *Journal of the History of Medicine & Allied Sciences* 18 (1963): 220-40.

A historical survey of commitment practices before the arrival of mental "diseases" and psychiatric "treatments."

Rothman, David J. *The discovery of the asylum: social order and disorder in the new republic*. Boston: Little, Brown & Co., 1971.

Shows how mental hospitals were not medical at first.

b) Thomas S. Szasz

Psychiatrist Thomas S. Szasz has been a prolific writer on psychiatry and the law since the mid-1950's. His writings present a systematic exposure of how the mental health system serves our scientific/technological society as an instrument for social control. According to Szasz, "mental illness" is a myth of our scientific ideology, a myth perpetuated for the purpose of manufacturing mental patients whom society can persecute as its scapegoat in much the same way as medieval Christianity persecuted its witches and heretics. He thus sees psychiatrists as our society's own "high priests", sanctioned to enforce its values and punish its heretics. Szasz also believes that the medical model is inappropriate to "problems in living", that involuntary treatment is unconstitutional, and that all persons in conflict with the law should be held legally responsible. The brand of psychiatric treatment he does preach is called "autonomous psychotherapy", and is based upon a voluntary contractual agreement between therapist and client.

Although Szasz helped found the American Association for the Abolition of Involuntary Mental Hospitalization (AAAIMH), he is generally regarded as more of a theorist than an activist. His influence frequently appears in the writings of other civil liberties-oriented psychiatrists such as Peter Breggin and E. Fuller Torrey.

Szasz is important to the mental patients liberation movement because his writings denounced the medical model of mental illness and helped open up the attack on involuntary treatment and related patients' rights issues. The main limitation of his work is that he does not go far enough in his social analysis; he fails to attack the larger capitalist structure.

i) Books

Szasz, Thomas S. *Pain and pleasure: a study of bodily feelings.* 2nd ed., expanded. New York: Basic Books, 1975.

Szasz, Thomas S. *The myth of mental illness: foundations of a theory of personal conduct.* Revised ed. New York: Harper & Row, 1974.

Reviews the history and psychology of hysteria to show how the medical model came to be applied to what is actually a "problem in living" and problem of symbolic communication, rather than an "illness".

Szasz, Thomas S. *Law, liberty and psychiatry: an inquiry into the social uses of mental health practices.* New York: Macmillan, 1963.

"This book has two major aims: first, to present a critical inquiry into the current social, and especially legal, uses of psychiatry; second, to offer a reasoned dissent from what I consider the theory and practice of false psychiatric liberalism."

Szasz, Thomas S. *The ethics of psychoanalysis: the theory and method of autonomous psychotherapy.* New York: Basic Books, 1965.

"In this book, I propose to describe psychotherapy as social action, not as healing . . . a contractual, rather than 'therapeutic' relationship between analyst and analysand . . . . In sum, I shall attempt to define the nature of psychoanalysis; clarify its limits; and establish ethics, and social science."

Szasz, Thomas S. *Psychiatric justice.* New York: Macmillan, 1965.

" . . . how the psychiatric profession and the legal establishment unwittingly conspire to deny citizens their constitutional right to trial . . . . Szasz attacks on Constitutional grounds the practice of involuntary pretrial psychiatric examination and subsequent 'hospitalization' . . . a fascinating glimpse into the inner workings of psychiatry in the courtroom . . . . " (from book jacket).

Szasz, Thomas S. *Ideology and insanity: essays on the psychiatric dehumanization of man.* Garden City, New York: Anchor Books, 1970.

A collection of essays, all but one having appeared earlier and slightly revised for this book. "What I have sought to capture here is but one feature, albeit an important one, of this modern, scientific-technological ideology, namely, the ideology of sanity and insanity, of mental health and mental illness."
Includes: Introduction, "The Myth of Mental Illness"; "The Mental Health Ethic"; "The Rhetoric of Rejection"; "Mental Health as Ideology"; "What Psychiatry Can and Cannot Do"; "Bootlegging Humanistic Values Through

Psychiatry"; "The Insanity Plea and the Insanity Verdict"; "Involuntary Mental Hospitalization: A Crime Against Humanity"; "Mental Health Services in the School"; "Psychiatric Classification as a Strategy of Personal Constraint"; "Whither Psychiatry".

Szasz, Thomas S. *The manufacture of madness: a comparative study of the Inquisition and the mental health movement*. New York: Dell, 1971.

"In the present work, I shall try to show how and why the ethical convictions and social arrangement based on this concept (the concept of mental illness) constitute an immoral ideology of intolerance. In particular, I shall compare the belief in witchcraft and the persecution of witches with the belief in mental illness and the persecution of mental patients."

Szasz, Thomas S. *The age of madness: the history of involuntary mental hospitalization, presented in selected texts.* See XI-b, Anthologies.

Szasz, Thomas S. *Ceremonial chemistry: the ritual persecution of drugs, addicts, and pushers*. Garden City, New York: Doubleday/Anchor, 1975.

How society's attitude towards drugs (pushing some, prohibiting others) belongs in the realm of religion and politics. That disapproved drugs, their users/pushers and their persecution belongs in the same class of scapegoat persecution as witches, Jews, and madpersons.

Szasz, Thomas S. *Heresies*. New York: Doubleday/Anchor, 1976.

Some iconoclastic thoughts on life, in the form of aphorisms.

Szasz, Thomas S. *Karl Kraus and the soul doctors: a pioneer critic and his criticism of psychiatry and psychoanalysis*. Baton Rouge, La.: Louisiana State University Press, 1976.

Szasz, Thomas S. *Schizophrenia: the sacred symbol of psychiatry*. New York: Basic Books, 1976.

Szasz attacks schizophrenia, psychiatry's most dreaded "mental illness". He critically examines chemical and other theories; concludes that schizophrenia is not a disease but the "sacred symbol of psychiatry".

Szasz, T.S. *Psychiatric slavery.* New York: Free Press, 1977.

Szasz, T.S. *The theology of medicine: the political-philosophical foundations of medical ethics.* New York: Harper & Row, 1977.

ii) Articles

Szasz has written several hundred articles: only a small representative sample is included here.

Szasz, T.S. "Some observations on the relationship between psychiatry and the law." *A.M.A. Archives of Neurology & Psychiatry* 75 (1956): 297.

Szasz, T.S. "Malingering: 'Diagnosis' or social condemnation? Analysis of the meaning of 'diagnosis' in the light of some interrlations of social structure, value judgment, and the physician's role." *A.M.A. Archives of Neurology & Psychiatry* 76 (1956): 432.

Szasz, T.S. "Commitment of the mentally ill: 'Treatment' or social restraint?" *Journal of Nervous & Mental Disorders* 125 (1957): 293-307.

Szasz, T.S. "A contribution to the psychology of schizophrenia.' *A.M.A. Archives of Neurology & Psychiatry* 77 (1957): 420-436.

Szasz, T.S. "Politics and mental health: some remarks apropos of the case of Mr. Ezra Pound." *American Journal of Psychiatry* 115 (1958): 508-11.

Szasz, T.S. "Psycho-analytic training: a sociopsychological analysis of its history and present status." *International Journal of Psycho-Analysis* 39 (1958): 598-613.

Szasz, T.S. "Scientific method and social role in medicine and psychiatry." *A.M.A. Archives of Internal Medicine* 101 (Feb. 1958): 228-238.

Szasz, T.S. "The ethics of birth control: or, who owns your body?" *Humanist* 20 (Nov.-Dec. 1960): 332-336.

Szasz, T.S. "A psychiatrist dissents from Durham." *Journal of Nervous and Mental Disease* (July 1960): 58-63.

Szasz, T.S. "Bootlegging humanistic values through psychiatry." *Antioch Review* 22 (Fall 1962): 341-349.

Szasz, T.S. "Legal and moral aspects of homosexuality." In *Sexual inversion: the multiple roots of homosexuality,* ed. by J. Marmor. New York: Basic Books, 1965.

Szasz, T.S. "Toward the therapeutic state." *New Republic* (Dec. 11, 1965): 26-29.

Szasz, T.S. "Mental illness is a myth." *New York Times Magazine* 30 (June 12, 1966): 90-92.

Szasz, T.S. "Psychotherapy: a sociocultural perspective." *Comprehensive Psychiatry* 7 (Aug. 1966): 217-223.

Szasz, T.S. "The psychiatrist as double agent." *Trans-Action* 4 (Oct. 1967): 16-24.

Szasz, T.S. "Medical ethics: a historical perspective." *Medical Opinion & Review* 4 (Feb. 1968): 115-121.

Szasz, T.S. "Science and public policy: the crime of involuntary mental hospitalization." *Medical Opinion & Review* 4 (May 1968): 24-35.

Szasz, T.S. "An 'unscrewtape' letter: a reply to Fred Sander." *American Journal of Psychiatry* 125 (Apr. 1969): 1432-5.

Szasz, T.S. "The sane slave. An historical note on the use of medical diagnosis as justificatory rhetoric." *American Journal of Psychotherapy* 25 (Apr. 1971): 228-39.

Szasz, T.S. "American Association for the Abolition of Involuntary Hospitalization." *American Journal of Psychiatry* 127 (June 1971): 1968.

Szasz, T.S. "The Negro in psychiatry. An historical note on psychiatric rhetoric." *American Journal of Psychotherapy* 25 (July 1971): 469-71.

Szasz, T.S. "Voluntary mental hospitalization. An unacknowledged practice of medical fraud." *New England Journal of Medicine* 287 (Aug. 1972): 277-8.

Szasz, T.S. "Illness and indignity." *Journal of the American Mental Association* 227 (Feb. 1974): 543-5.

Szasz, T.S. "Psychiatry: a clear and present danger." *Mental Hygiene* 58 (Spring 1974): 17-20.

Szasz, T.S. "Might makes the metaphor." *Journal of the American Medical Association* 229 (Sept. 1974): 1326.

Szasz, T.S. & Alexander, G.J. "Law, property, and psychiatry." *American Journal of Orthopsychiatry* 42 (July 1972): 610-26.

Szasz, T.S. & Hollender, M.H. "A contribution to the philosophy of medicine. The basic models of the doctor-patient relationship." *A.M.A. Archives of Internal Medicine* 97 (1956): 585.

Szasz, T.S., Knoff, W.F. & Hollender, M.H. "The doctor-patient relationship in its historical context." *American Journal of Psychiatry* 115 (1958):522-8.

iii) Outside Criticisms and Reviews

Breggin, P.R. "Psychotherapy as applied ethics." *Psychiatry* 34 (February 1971): 59-74.

This article centers around a discussion of "autonomous psychotherapy" and includes, among other things, a short presentation of and commentary on Szasz's system of psychiatry.

Glaser, F.G. "The dichotomy game: a further consideration of the writings of Dr. Thomas Szasz." *American Journal of Psychiatry* 121 (May 1965): 1069-74.

Guttmacher, M.S. "Critique of views of Thomas Szasz on legal psychiatry." *A.M.A. Archives of General Psychiatry* 10 (March 1964): 238-45.

Kubie, L.S. "The myths of Thomas Szasz." *Bull, Menniger Clinic* 38(6) (November 1974): 497-502.

Moss, G.R. "Szasz: review and criticism." *Psychiatry* 31 (1968): 184-94.

Reiss, S. "A critique of Thomas S. Szasz's 'Myth of Mental Illness'." *American Journal of Psychiatry* 128 (March 1972): 1081-5.

Sander, F.M. "Some thoughts on Thomas Szasz." *American Journal of Psychiatry* 125 (April 1969): 1429-31.

Siegler, Miriam and Osmond, Humphrey. *Models of madness, models of medicine*. New York: Macmillan, 1974.

This books analyzes models currently in psychiatric use and attacks Szasz for his rejection of medical model.

c) Other Related Writings on Political/Legal Aspects of Psychiatry

Further information about the political machinery of psychotherapy can be found in VI, Professionalism and the Mental Health Industry.

Breggin, P.R. "Psychotherapy as applied ethics." *Psychiatry* 34 (February 1971): 59-74.

Discusses theory and ethics of Szasian "autonomous psychotherapy". Like Szasz, Breggin views therapy as a contractual arrangement between client and therapist operating within a political system of free enterprise. Breggin has also made some important contributions to the fight against psychosurgery and other forms of enforced mind control: for more of his writings, see V-b, Psychosurgery; IV-b, Prisons; I-b, General Fiction.

Breggin, P.R. "The politics of therapy." *Mental Hygiene* 56 (Summer 1972): 9-12.

Breggin, P.R. "Psychiatry and psychotherapy as political processes." *American Journal of Psychotherapy* 29(3) (July 1975): 369-82.

Argues that psychotherapy must be seen not only as applied ethics (as Szasz does), but also as applied politics. Includes discussion of problems of socialist orientation alongside the free-enterprise foundation of autonomous psychotherapy.

Hess, John H. and Thomas, Herbert E. "Incompetency to stand trial: procedures, results, and problems." *American Journal of Psychiatry* 119 (February 1963): 713-20.

An early empirical study of psychiatric determination of competence. Shows how being declared unfit to stand trial is used as punishment.

Kittrie, N.N. *The right to be different: deviance and enforced therapy*. Baltimore: John Hopkins Press, 1971.

Well documented study "considers all types of deviant individuals, showing that such people often express greater fear of imposed therapy than of criminal justice." (Book cover). Includes proposal for a new therapeutic bill of rights to guard individual liberty against unbridled therapeutic enthusiasm.

Kutner, Luis. "The illusion of due process in commitment proceedings." *Northwestern University Law Review* 57 (September 1962): 383-99. (Also included in T.J. Scheff, *Mental Illness and Social Processes*.)

Describes commitment procedures in Chicago in 1962, where "certificates are signed as a matter of course by staff physicians after little or no examination . . . the doctors recommend confinement in 77 per cent of the cases. It appears in practice that the alleged mentally-ill is presumed to be insane and bears the burden of proving his sanity in the few minutes allowed to him."

Leifer, Ronald. *In the name of mental health: the social functions of psychiatry*. New York: Science House, 1969.

Written by an M.D.; along the lines of Szasz.

Martindale, Don and Martindale, Edith. *Psychiatry and the law: the crusade against involuntary hospitalization*. St. Paul: Windflower, 1973.

Critical historical review of the movement in the early 1970's to abolish involuntary mental hospitalization in the United States.

Scheff, Thomas J. "The societal reaction to deviance: ascriptive elements in the psychiatric screening of mental patients in a Midwestern State." *Social Problems* 11 (Spring 1964): 401-13.

This study into commitment proceedings finds that "in the face of uncertainty, there is a strong presumption of illness by the court and the court psychiatrist".

Swadron, Barry B. and Sullivan, Donald R., eds. *The law and mental disorder*. Toronto: Canadian Mental Health Association, 1973.

"A comprehensive edition of the report of the Committee on Legislation and Psychiatric Disorder: a committee of the National Scientific Planning Council of the Canadian Mental Health Association." Critically examines mental health legislation in Canada.

d) Patient's Rights

The struggle for patient's rights is central to the anti-psychiatry movement because, although the movement's ultimate goal is to smash/eliminate the present mental health system, it is crucial in the meantime to work towards protecting people's rights within the system.

Mental health laws have been changing. In California and Washington for instance, non-dangerous persons are no longer supposed to be stashed away indefinetely in mental hospitals. There seems to be a general trend towards emptying mental hospitals and sending their inmates out into the community; however, some of these changes are no more than government schemes to lower spending on mental health care. And in most cases, changes are small - in Canada, for example, patient's rights have yet to be spelled out and are virtually non-existent.

Mental Patients liberation groups and civil liberties groups are involved throughout the world in struggles to change mental health laws as well as insuring that existing rights are protected. The American Civil Liberties Union is involved in litigation test cases. Other groups have been designing new model mental health acts to submit before legislatures; still others are compiling patient's rights handbooks, or setting up ombudservices in mental hospitals.

Running hot on the trail of any progressive changes is a strong counter-movement by reactionary forces seeking to undo any gains and bring in a little further repression for good measure. One thing working to their advantage is the frequently vague wording of mental health bills and special "emergency" clauses appended to them that allows for arbitrary interpretation by the people administering the laws.

Good up-to-date coverage of the gains and losses in the legal struggle can be found in issues of *Madness Network News* and *State and Mind*, as well as newsletters put out by most movement groups.

Boggan, E. et al. *The rights of gay people.* New York: Avon/Discus, 1975.

This American Civil Liberties Handbook summarizes, from state to state, what basic rights are granted or denied gay people.

Boston MPLF. *Your rights as a mental patient in Massachusetts.* Available for $2 (or free if you need a copy but can't afford it) from: Mental Patients Liberation Front, Box 156, Somerville, Ma. 02144, U.S.A.

Dobson, Grant and Hansen, R.C. "The ombudsman in mental health: Lakeshore's experience." *Canada's Mental Health* 24(3) (September 1976): 11-13.

Donaldson, Kenneth. *Insanity inside out*. See I-a, Autobiographical Accounts.

Ennis, Bruce. *Prisoners of psychiatry: mental patients, psychiatrists, and the law*. New York: Avon/Discus, 1972.

Based upon a litigation project (Mental Health Law Project) started by New York Civil Liberties Union in December 1968, to protect and expand the rights of mental patients. About author's experiences defending mental patients; good for test cases. Also about what happens to people who get locked away in mental institutions.

Ennis, Bruce and Siegel, Loren. *The rights of mental patients: the basic ACLU guide to mental patients' rights*. New York: R.V. Baron, 1973.

"An indispensible book for mental patients and others working to secure mental patients' rights . . . easy to read information . . . each state's laws and methods of fighting the hospitals and psychiatrists in court . . . . From involuntary commitment to free legal service to shock treatment . . . contains a bibliography for looking up more detailed information . . . to mention the drawbacks . . . . Since it is an American Civil Liberties project, the book does not take strong political stands, although the anti-institutional psychiatry position is clear. . . ." (Review, *Rough Times* 3(6))

Ettlinger, R.A. "Advocate informs patients of rights and responsibilities." *Hospital & Community Psychiatry* 24 (July 1973): 465.

Friedman, Paul R. *The rights of mentally retarded persons.* New York: Avon, 1977.

American Civil Liberties Handbook. Discusses problems of classifications, commitment, rights within institutions, rights in the community, and rights in the criminal process. Includes list of resource organizations.

Greenblatt, M. "Class action and the right to treatment." *Hospital & Community Psychiatry* 25 (July 1974): 449-52.

Hancen, C. "The rights of mental patients: a civil libertarian replies." *Hospital & Community Psychiatry* 26(4) (April 1975): 232-3.

Hooper, Jackie. "Citizen advocacy and MPA." *In a Nutshell: Mental Patients Association Newsletter* 4(3), July 1976.

Points out how, at present, even the most basic rights of patients confined in mental hospitals are not yet spelled out in British Columbia mental health legislation. Says that some form of citizen advocacy or ombudsperson would provide at least a temporary solution.

How to cope with the Mental Health Act 1959. See XI-c: Pamphlets, etc.

Jansen, D.S. "Personality characteristics of a state hospital patients' rights office visitors." *Journal of Clinical Psychology* 30 (July 1974): 347-9.

Jansen, D.G. and Krause, L.J. "The nature of complaints of inpatients who visit a patients' rights office." *Hospital and Community Psychiatry* 25 (July 1974): 446-8.

Johnson, B. and Aanes, D. "Patients' use of a full-time patient advocate office in a state hospital." *Hospital & Community Psychiatry* 25 (July 1974): 445-6.

Legal Authority and Mental Patient Status (LAMP) Information Packet. See XI-c, Pamphlets.

LAMP Notes. Column in *Madness Network News.* See XI-e, Periodicals.

Regular feature by the Center for the Study of Legal Authority and Mental Patient Status (see Appendix B-a-ii, Directory, "LAMP"). Discusses news about legal issues relating to mental patients.

LaPlante, Joseph A. "Conneticut Criminal Law: deficiencies disclosed in the Reid Case." *Conneticut Bar Journal* 37 (March 1963): 17-51.

Legal Advocacy programs for the mentally disabled: a preliminary survey and directory. Booklet. Available from: American Bar Association Commission on the Mentally Disabled, 1800 M Street N.W., Washington, D.C. 20036, U.S.A.

Prepared for the National Committee on Patients Rights. Includes listing of several hundred agencies and organizations around the U.S. interested in legal advocacy services.

Meisel, A. "Rights of the mentally ill: the gulf between theory and reality." *Hospital & Community Psychiatry* 26(6) (June 1975): 349-53.

Mental Patients and the Law. (Booklet) Available from:Vancouver People's Law School, Ste. 610-207 W. Hastings St., Vancouver, B.C. V6B 1H7, Canada.

The School regularly offers free courses on Mental Patients and the Law which are three evenings long each, and also shorter Sunday afternoon seminars. Phone (604)681-7532 for information and to pre-register.

M.P.A. Revised Mental Health Act. See X-b, Vancouver Mental Patients Association.

The mental patients' handbook of legal rights in Ohio. Pamphlet. Newly revised. Available from: Patients' Rights Organization (see Appendix B-a for address).

Morrison, James K. "An argument for mental patient advisory boards." *Professional Psychology* (May 1976): 127-31.

Morrison is becoming a prolific writer on client input to mental health clinics. This article is the first in a series that he is planning to publish; it includes a bibliography. For reprints, or further communication, write: James K. Morrison, Capitol District Psychiatric Center, 169 Mohawk Street, Cohoes, New York 12047, U.S.A.

National Association of Mental Health position on civil rights of mental patients. *Mental Hygiene* 56 (Spring 1972): 67-9.

New York Mental Patients Liberation Front. "A mental patients liberation project: Statement and Bill of Rights." In *Rough Times,* ed. by J. Agel. New York: Ballantine, 1973. (Also included in *The radical therapist*, Penguin edition.)

Page, S. "Toward evaluating the meaningfulness of legal counsel for psychiatric patients." *Canada's Mental Health* 24(3) (September 1976): 6-10.

Peele, R. "Litigation as a means of improving treatment: is it the best approach?" *Hospital and Community Psychiatry* 26 (March 1975): 170-1.

Potts, Jim. *Self-help litigation manual.* Available (free to prisoners) from: National Prison Project (A.C.L.U.). See Appendix B-c, Other Groups, for address.

Prisoners' rights handbook. An updated version of the old American Civil Liberties manual. Available (free to prisoners) from: National Prison Project (A.C.L.U.). See Appendix B-c, Other Groups, for address.

Rachlin, S. "With liberty and psychosis for all." *Psychiatry Quarterly* 48(3) (1974): 410-20.

Rachlin, S. et. al. "Civil liberties versus involuntary hospitalization." *American Journal of Psychiatry* 132(2) (February 1975): 189-92.

Revitch, E. et. al. "Letter: More on 'Dying with their rights on'." *American Journal of Psychiatry* 131(11) (November 1974): 1289-1320.

Rouse, L.L., Hood, W. and Allen, L.T. "Patient Council." *American Journal of Public Health* 61(12) (December 1971): 2383-6.

This important paper documents how a successful prototype patients' council was formed in a Detroit hospital for TB. Shows how a group of patients organized and struggled against the directors of the medical hierarchy. The authors conclude that: "We recommend our model of purposefully employing and involving consumers of health services in the health team as a means of bridging the gap that currently exists. We also recommend the involvement of consumers, not only through employment, but as consulting and cooperative participators in health program policy, planning, and administration. This type of consumer involvement seems to have potential for more relevant, sensitive and community related services."

Schmolling, P. "Civil rights for mental patients: the road to neglect?" *Hospital and Community Psychiatry* 26 (March 1975): 168-70.

Schwartz, L.H. "Litigating the right to treatment." *Hospital and Community Psychiatry* 25 (July 1974): 460-3.

Silverberg, H.M. "Letter: 'Dying with their rights on'." *American Journal of Psychiatry* 131 (June 1974): 725.

Stickney, S.B. "Problems in implementing the right to treatment in Alabama: the Wyall vs. Stickney case." *Hospital and Community Psychiatry* 25 (July 1974): 453-60.

Strand, David. "Legal aid for patients in state mental institutions: the Cleveland experience." *Clearinghouse Review* 6(8). December 1972.

An informative article on legal aspects of patients' rights, commitment law, and other important areas. Ties together social critiques of Goffman and Szasz with legal progress in mental health areas.

Tancredi, L. *Legal issues in psychiatric care*. New York: Harper & Row, 1975.

Thompson, B. and Hall, J. "Helping psychiatric inpatients exercise their right to vote." *Hospital and Community Psychiatry* 25 (July 1974): 441-5.

Thorner, N. "Nurses violate their patients rights" *Journal of Psychiatric Nursing* 14(1) (January 1976): 7-12.

Treffert, D.A. "Dying with their rights on." *American Journal of Psychiatry* 130 (September 1973): 1041.

IV. Psychiatry and
Institutions

IV PSYCHIATRY AND INSTITUTIONS

These writings unveil the repressive operations of institutional psychiatry. They show how mental hospitals and prisons function as "human warehouses" for confining non-cooperative workers, housewives, ghetto residents, etc. Documenting psychiatric abuse in its many guises (all euphemistically named "therapy"), they show how it is used by these institutions to mystify, control, punish, and torture inmates. While reading these works it becomes apparent how the two types of institutions are becoming increasingly similar to each other.

As would be expected, racism and sexism run rampant in these places. Inmate populations are drawn from the lower socio-economic classes. (For further documentation and analysis, see sections VII, Psychiatry and Women and VIII, Psychiatry and Other Oppressed Groups.)

The list of abuses now under attack by inmates' movement groups is extensive; it includes: forced drugging of inmates, use of electroshock and other torture methods as punishment, slave labour, use of inmates as human "guinea pigs" for biomedical experimentation, and indeterminate confinement for inmates who won't conform.

For further accounts of what goes on in these institutions, see sections I, The Mental Patient Experience and V, Mind Control Technology.

a) Mental Hospitals

In contrast to the inmates' descriptions of life in a mental hospital which are listed in I-a, Autobiographical Accounts, the writings in this section are mainly studies by sociologists and journalists. Many of them, such as Goffman's *Asylums* and the famous Rosenhaun study, examine the social structure of mental hospitals; their observations tear apart many prevailing psychiatric myths and show how these institutions are actually "counter-therapeutic". Other works expose how people who won't conform are railroaded into mental hospitals and imprisoned there: Elizabeth P. Ware Packard's *Modern Persecution* and Szasz's *The Age of Madness* are comprehensive historical documents, while Bruce Ennis, the Braginskys, and others give a picture of modern psychiatric imprisonment.

Barry, Anne. *Bellevue is a state of mind*. New York: Harcourt, Brace & Jovanovich, 1971.

Journalist signed herself into Bellevue for a week.

Braginsky, B.M., Braginsky, D.D. and Ring, K. *Methods of madness: the mental hospital as a last resort*. See II-b, Other Social/Phenomenological Studies.

Braginsky, D. D. and Braginsky, B.M. *Hansels and Gretals: studies of children in institutions*. New York: Holt, Rinehart & Winston, 1971.

Brandt, Anthony. *Reality police: the experience of insanity in America*. New York: William Morrow & Co., 1975.

Good primer for people unfamiliar with psychiatric scene. Written by a journalist who signed himself in and was soon denied his individual interests by institution. Pokes holes in the psychiatric model.

Brown, Phil. "Social change at Harrowdale State Hospital: Impression 2." In *Rough times*, ed. by J. Agel. New York: Ballantine, 1973.

A first-hand report of some important first steps taken in a mental hospital's programme to free it up.

Critical Mass Gallery. See XI-d, Audio-Visual.

Ennis, Bruce J. *Prisoners of psychiatry: mental patients, psychiatrists, and the law*. See III-d. Patients' Rights.

The Fairview papers. Available for $3 ($2 to ex-and current psychiatric inmates) from: Alliance for the Liberation of Mental Patients (see Appendix B-a for address).

An eighty-six page report (once secret) of the Pennsylvania Attorney General's 1975 investigation into abuses at Fairview State Hospital for the Criminally Insane. Contains evidence of shocking brutality.

Ganung, Cynthia. "Social change at Harrowdale State Hospital: Impression I." In *Rough times*, ed. by J. Agel. New York: Ballantine, 1973.

Goffman, Erving. *Asylums: essays on the social situation of mental patients and other inmates*. New York: Doubleday/Anchor, 1961.

Classic document on the social dynamic of mental institutions. ". . . It is the thesis of this book that the most important factor in forming a mental-hospital patient is his institution, not his illness, and that his reactions and adjustments are those of inmates in other types of total institutions as well." (from book jacket review)

Hirsch, Sherry, Adams, Joe Kennedy, et al. *Madness network news reader*. See XI-b, Anthologies.

Madness Network News. An important source of regular news features about mental institutions and the movement's struggle against them in all areas, including lobbying against the unpaid labour situation. See XI-e, Periodicals.

Packard, Elizabeth P. Ware. *Modern persecution; or, insane asylums unveiled, as demonstrated by the Report of the Investigating Committee of the Legislature of Illinois*, 2 volumes in 1, reprinted from the 1875 edition. New York: Arno Press, 1973.

Classic historical work describing the conditions of institutional psychiatry and commitment proceedings during the 19th century. Cites case studies to illustrate points. Packard was a 19th century activist following her incarceration by husband and doctor. She was the first person to make the analogy between institutional psychiatry and the Inquisition (which was later picked up and expanded by T.S. Szasz). Packard's case is one of those discussed in Chesler's *Women and Madness* (see VII-a, Women: General Works).

Packard, Elizabeth P. Ware. *Great disclosure of spiritual wickedness in high places: with appeal to the government to protect the inalienable rights of women.* Reprinted from the 1865 edition. New York: Arno Press, 1974.

Perruci, Robert. *Circles of madness: on being insane and institutionalized in America*. Englewood Cliffs, New Jersey: Prentice-Hall/Spectrum, 1974.

A sociology of life in mental hospital, observed firsthand. Argues for release of non-dangerous inmates.

Rosenhaun, David. "On being sane in insane places." *Science* 179 (1973): 250-8.

Classic study exposing some psychiatric myths. A group of "pseudo-patients" were admitted to mental hospital and events which followed led Rosenhaun to conclude that: "It is clear that we cannot distinguish the sane from the insane in psychiatric hospitals."

Szasz, Thomas S. *The age of madness: the history of involuntary mental hospitalization presented in selected texts*. These articles give excellent glimpse into the workings of mental hospitals, past and present. See XI-b, Anthologies.

Vail, David J. *Dehumanization and the institutional career*. Springfield: Charles C. Thomas, 1966.

Late medical director of Minnesota's mental hospital system takes a critical look at institutions. Vail was an early supporter of Szasz and the American Association for the Abolition of Involuntary Mental Hospitalization when it started; he helped launch the Minnesota phase of the crusade against involuntary committal.

Weisblat, Vicki L. "An overall view of today's mental hospital." In *Toward social change: a handbook for all those who will*, ed. by R. Buckhout and 81 Concerned Berkley Students. New York: Harper & Row, 1971.

A representative first-hand account written by university student volunteer at mental hospital. Concludes with suggestion that mental hospitals and medical/psychiatric frame of reference be abolished.

b) Prisons

These works document the rise of psychiatry in prisons. The current trend is toward constructing special psychiatric units ("adjustment centers") for the indeterminate confinement of non-cooperative prisoners. Psychiatric prison centers such as those at Vacaville, Patuxent, and Marion have received a lot of attention from American anti-psychiatry writers. These places have enjoyed a broad arsenal of mind control techniques to punish and subdue the aggressive violent inmate including drugging, behavior mod, sensory deprivation, brainwashing, and psychosurgery.

Groups such as the National Committee to Support the Marion Brothers and the ACLU National Prison Project have been working to fight the increasing psychiatric abuse of prisoners in the United States (see Appendix B-c, Other Groups).

In other parts of the world, psychiatric repression of political prisoners is flourishing. The most publicized example has been the Soviet Union. Junta dictatorships in Latin America are also using psychiatric methods to torture their political prisoners (see VIII-d, Political Dissidents).

Articles on prisons and massive federal mind control program for prisoners. *Rough Times* 3(5) 1973.

Bar None. This prison-support paper has special back issues on "Women in Prison" and "Gay Prisoners". Available from: Bar None, P.O. Box 124, West Somerville, Mass. 02144, U.S.A.

Breaking men's minds: behavior control and human experimentation at the Federal Prison in Marion, Illinois. Pamphlet. Written by former inmate of Marion control unit. Available free (though donations are welcomed) from: National Committee to Support the Marion Brothers (see Appendix B-c for address).

Coleman, Lee. "Prisons: the crime of treatment." *Psychiatric Opinion* 11(3) (June 1974): 5-16.

Coleman applies Szaszian principles to prison system.

Committee for the Defense of Soviet Political Prisoners. *Inside Soviet prisons*. Pamphlet. New York: C.D.S.P.P. Press, 1976. Available from: P.O. Box 142, Cooper Station, New York, N.Y. 10003, U.S.A.

Federal Prisoners Coalition. "Brainwashing U.S. Prisoners." *Rough Times* 3(4) (1973): 6-7.

"This letter to the U.N. details the introduction of social psychology techniques for control of U.S. prisoners. These techniques are based on the work of Edgar Schein, whose papers on 'brainwashing' are included in every major collection of readings in social psychology for college students." (from *RT's* commentary)

Good Times/Liberation News Service. "Vacaville: lobotomies, shock therapy and torture for 'violent' California prisoners." In *Rough times*, ed. by J. Agel. New York: Ballantine, 1973.

Describes new "intensive psychiatric prison center" being set up at Vacaville State Mental Facility to control "the aggressive, destructive, political inmate."

Instead of prisons: a handbook for abolitionists. Available for $6.50 plus $.50 postage from: Prison Research Education Action Project, c/o Safer Society Press, 3049 E. Genesee St., Syracuse, N.Y. 13224, U.S.A.

Liberation News Service. "Not a prison nor a mental institution." *Rough Times* 3(4) (1973): 4-5.

About Maryland's Patuxent Institution: a prison for those "in conflict with authority figures".

Lundy, Phyllis and Breggin, Peter R. "Psychiatric oppression of prisoners." *Psychiatric Opinion* 11(3) (June 1974): 30-7.

Examines current scene of prison psychiatry. Exposes how prison system employs psychiatrists to provide theory that will justify psychiatric tortures and therapy programmes to control and punish prisoners. Condemns these practices as "punishment in the guise of therapy."

McConnell, James V. "Criminals can be brainwashed—now." *Psychology Today* 3(11), April, 1970. (Also reprinted in *Toward social change: a handbook for those who will*, ed. by R. Buckhout et. al. New York: Harper & Row, 1971.)

McNeil, Gerard with Vance, Sharon. *Cruel and unusual*. Toronto: Denean & Greenberg, 1978.

This book came out of the tour of the Commons Subcommitee on the Penitentiary System in Canada. It reveals the shocking reality of life behind bars in Canada.

Mitford, Jessica. *Kind and unusual punishment: the prison business*. New York: Random House/Vintage Books, 1974.

Mitford's comprehensive study of oppression inside prisons. Contains section on psychiatric treatment of prisoners. Includes directory of organizations and publications for prisoners' rights.

Myers, Scott W. "Brainwash and whitewash: battling the new Alcatraz at Marion." *State and Mind* 5(5) March-April, 1977.

Prison Issue. *Madness Network News* 2(5) 1975.

Resources for Community Change. *Women behind bars*. Booklet.

An organizing tool produced in 1975. Contains articles; legal information; listings of groups, resources, newspapers, bibliographies, etc. Available for $1.75 from: Resources for Community Change, P.O. Box 21066, Washington, D.C. 20009, U.S.A.

Whalen, Eileen. "Women in prisons." *Rough Times* 3(4), 1973.

Describes the current situation of women locked up in prisons; gives listing of some New York women's prison projects (The Women's Bail Fund, Committee on Women Prisoners, Women's Prison Committee, Freedom to Read for Women Prisoners).

Women Locked Up. Special issue of *Women, A Journal of Liberation* 3(3).

Contains stories of women in prisons, hospitals, and other institutions that oppress us. Available for $1.00 from : *Women, A Journal of Liberation*, 3028 Greenmount Ave., Baltimore, Md. 21218, U.S.A.

V. Mind Control
Technology
ECT
ECG ECG

V MIND CONTROL TECHNOLOGY

In psychiatry today, the trend is toward an ever-increasing use of mind control technology. This technology has many facets – drugging, adverse therapy, violence screening, psychosurgery, to name a few – all of which are rising in both sophistication and popularity. These weapons of psychiatric violence have also been moving into non-medical areas, prisons and schools in particular. Everywhere, their purpose is the same: to modify and control behavior. These techniques have become widely implemented over the past 25 or so years; they have been responsible for changing the "raving lunatic" atmosphere of the cruder old-style mental (and other) institutions into a seemingly more sane, orderly, and clinical one where the inmates are more pacified and docile.

These techniques fall roughly into "hard" and "soft" categories. The "hard" ones – electroshock, drugging, psychosurgery – all produce some degree of destruction of healthy brain tissue, either directly by cutting with a knife or indirectly through cumulative side-effects from drug poisoning and electrical "frying". The "soft" techniques – screening, behavior mod, etc. – stem largely from modern research advances of psychologists and other social scientists. They include snooping into people's lives and collecting "dossiers", brainwashing, sensory deprivation, and punishment (torture).

The majority of subjects for these expanding technologies are drawn from target populations of mental patients, women, prisoners, political dissidents, third world persons, and children. But all workers/consumers are now vulnerable to mind control technology's intervention in their lives through such widespread practices as I.Q. tests; mass media advertising is another facet of "soft" control.

There exists abundant financial backing for research programs to develop and implement this technology much further; the money presently flows in from both government and wealthy corporate sources.

References in this section reveal some of the truth – scientific, political, economic – behind these current psychotechnological "treatments" and related applications.

a) Principles of Mind Control and Brainwashing: Some Basic Texts

Some basic works (by professionals) which explore empirical and theoretical backgrounds of mind control.

Delgado, Jose. *Physical control of the brain: toward a psychocivilized society*. New York: Harper & Row, 1969.

About ESB (Electrical Stimulation of the Brain) and current work being done to perfect an electronic technology of mind control. One of the uses ESB has been put to by Delgado is to make patients friendly, loving, and "happier".

Frank, Jerome D. *Persuasion and healing: a comparative study of psychotherapy*. (rev. ed.) New York: Schocken, 1974.

Discusses religious healing, political (communist) thought reform, various schools of psychotherapy and psychoanalysis; shows how indoctrination and the healing process occur. Presents model for underlying process common to all of these activities.

Sargent, William. *Battle for the mind: a physiology of conversion and brain-washing*. London: Pan Books, 1957.

Describes the process whereby beliefs can be implanted in the human brain through religion, politics, and psychotherapy. His model is built upon the work of Pavlov.

Torrey, E. Fuller. *The mind game: witchdoctors and psychiatrists.* See VI, Professionalism and the Mental Health Industry.

Valenstein, Elliot S. *Brain control: a critical examination of brain stimulation and psychosurgery*. New York: John Wiley & Sons, 1973.

Reviews the history of psychosurgery, including classic animal experiments. Discusses ethical and social considerations, making suggestions for patients' rights, etc.

b) Psychosurgery

Psychosurgery is the willful destruction of healthy brain tissue for the purpose of modifying feeling or behavior. The traditional operation, frontal lobotomy, was introduced in 1936 by Dr. Walter Freeman and involves cutting of part of the brain's front section – the part which controls the so-called higher functions of reasoning, insight, creativity, etc. Between the mid-thirties and mid-fifties, lobotomies were performed on about 50,000 Americans, mostly state mental patients. (Lobotomy has also been widely used elsewhere – Canada, Europe, etc.) This operation was used mainly as a means of subduing violent "hopeless cases". Besides rendering these patients docile, it also destroyed their intellects, ambitions, and personalities. In the mid-fifties the use of lobotomy fell into disrepute, largely because of the meteoric success of new major tranquilizers in controlling disturbed mental patients.

Yet this decade has seen a rising return of interest in psychosurgery, both lobotomy and other more "refined" brain operations such as amygalatotomy and cingulotomy. Three leaders of this new wave are psychosurgeons Frank Ervin, Vernon Mark, and William Sweet who, in 1967, recommended "violence screening" of the ghettos to pick out potential rioters and give them psychosurgical "treatment". Their organization, the Neuro Foundation of Boston, has received impressive grants from organizations such as the U.S. Justice Department's Law Enforcement Assistance Administration and the National Institute of Mental Health.

One major application of psychosurgery being explored during its current revival is usage in prison "adjustment centers" for "violent" inmates. Psychosurgery also formed part of the CIA's investigations into uses of psychiatric techniques in intelligence work. Another recent milestone for the new wave of psychosurgery is the 1977 Report of the U.S. National Commission for the Protection of Human Subjects in Biomedical and Behavioral Research, which came out in favor of psychosurgery for involuntary mental patients, prisoners, and children.

Psychiatrist Peter Breggin has been documenting this new rise in psychosurgery and actively campaigning against it. Mental patients liberation groups such as Network Against Psychiatric Assault have also been very active in this area, leading demonstrations, lobbying, and disseminating information to educate the public. And on November 5, 1977, the American mental patients liberation movement held its first nation-wide day of protest against psychosurgery.

Beam, Joanna. *Sexism in psychosurgery*. Article reprint included in *LAMP Information Packet*. See XI-c, Pamphlets.

Breggin, Peter. *Information about psychosurgery and its abuses.* Write to: Peter Breggin, the Center for the Study of Psychiatry, 1827 - 19th St. N.W. Washington D.C. 20009, U.S.A.

Breggin, a Washington psychiatrist, is an important critic of the current uses of psychosurgery as means of social control. He engages in research to gather information on the abuses of psychosurgery and make it available to the public. Breggin is also a crusader against involuntary mental hospitalization, critical of the uses of psychiatry to oppress prisoners, and author of the novel *The Crazy From the Sane* (see I-b, General Fiction), which analyzes mental institutions in terms of Szasian dialectic. For Breggin's writings on "autonomous psychotherapy" see III-c, Psychiatry and the Law: Other Writings on Political/Legal Aspects of Psychiatry.

Breggin, Peter. "Psychosurgery for the control of violence – including a critical examination of the work of Vernon Mark and Frank Ervin." *Congressional Record,* March 30, 1972.

Breggin, Peter. "Lobotomies: an alert." *American Journal of Psychiatry* 129 (July 1972): 97-8.

Breggin, Peter. "Is psychosurgery on the upswing?" *Human Events*, May 5, 1973.

Breggin, Peter. "Follow-up study of Thomas R." *Rough Times* 3(8), 1973.

An independent follow-up on a person operated upon for violence and epilepsy by Drs. Vernon Mark, Frank Ervin, and William Sweet of the Boston Neuro-Research Foundation.

Breggin, Peter. "The second wave." *Mental Hygiene* 57(11), Winter, 1973.

Breggin, P.R. "Letter:Psychosurgery." *Journal of the American Medical Association* 226 (November 1973): 1121.

Breggin, Peter. "Underlying a method. Is psychosurgery an acceptable treatment for hyperactivity in children?" *Mental Hygiene* 58 (Winter, 1974): 19-21.

Coles, Gerald S. "Psychosurgery: too much thinking can cause emotional distress." *State and Mind* 5(5) March-April 1977.

An analysis of the 1976 Report on the Use of Psychosurgery by the National Commission for the Protection of Human Subjects of Biomedical and Behavioral Research.

Frank, Leonard R. "Peter Breggin visits the Bay Area." *Madness Network News*, 2(1), January, 1974.

About Breggin and his work in the fight against psychosurgery.

Hunt, Joe. "The politics of psychosurgery." *Rough Times* 3(7) 1973.

Discusses some of the current controversies in psychosurgery.

Hunt, Joe. "The politics of psychosurgery II." *Rough Times* 3(8), 1973.

A continuation of Hunt's article.

IRT Collective. "Special Psychosurgery Section." *Issues in Radical Therapy* 1(4), October 1973.

Liberation News Service. "Lobotomies and prison revolts." In *Rough times,* ed. by J. Agel. New York: Ballantine, 1973.

A letter to the State of California Department of Corrections from Robert L. Lawson, California Council on Criminal Justice, outlining a "Proposal for the Neurosurgical Treatment of Violent Inmates."

Liberation News Service. "Lobotomies are back." In *Rough times,* ed. by J. Agel. New York: Ballantine, 1973.

"Violence on the Brain: Use of Lobotomies in U.S. on the rise." Discusses current developments in lobotomy plus a few quotes from Breggin's critiques.

"Lobotomist List." *Madness Network News.* Column.

A new feature beginning towards the end of 1978 and modeled along the lines of *MNN*'s "Shock Doctor Roster" (see V-c, Shock Treatment). Names appearing in this list will be "people who willfully destroy brain tissue for the purpose of altering feeling or behavior. Electrode implants and ultrasound count. Stereotactic target shooters. . ." *MNN* requests readers to send in names and hospital affiliations of lobotomists, stating whether or not they are still destroying brains. They do not, however, publish information from anonymous sources.

Psychosurgery Pamphlets. Can be obtained from: M.C.H.R., 1151 Massachusetts Ave., Cambridge, Mass. 02138, U.S.A.

The Psychosurgery Committee of the Massachusetts Chapter of the Medical Committee for Human Rights has prepared two pamphlets which are available to people wanting more information about the "new psychosurgery": 1. *Violence Upon the Brain* is an essay with analysis, explanations, diagrams, glossary, appendices, and references. Price: $ .25 plus $ .12 postage.

2) *Psychosurgery and Its Abuses Today* is their psychosurgery packet, a collection of reprinted articles on psychosurgery from various places, including medical journals, underground newspapers, and the *Congressional Record.* Price: $1 plus postage.

"The return of lobotomy." *Congressional Record,* Feb. 24, 1973. Available from: 1735 K Street N.W., Washington, D.C. 20006, U.S.A.

c) Shock Treatment

The first electroshock treatment was administered by Ugo Cerletti to an Italian prisoner in 1938. Since then, this procedure has come to be routinely used in most mental institutions. Electro-convulsive therapy or ECT, as it is now called, has been used on just about every type of "mental illness", and is especially regarded as the treatment of choice for severe depressions. Two-thirds of all shock recipients are women.

Although ECT is now the most widely used form of shock treatment, other techniques have also been employed. Their common feature is inducing a state of coma lasting for several minutes to several hours after the shock. Insulin shock, an older form, involved administering insulin to reduce blood sugar levels, thereby depressing metabolic processes in the brain and producing a prolonged coma. In electroshock treatment, 70 to 170 volts of electricity are applied to the brain, via electrodes, for a fraction of a second. This causes seizure-like convulsions and coma resulting in amnesia. The administration of ECT is preceeded by a curare-like muscle relaxant to produce near-paralysis (to reduce the risk of bone dislocations and fractures) plus an anaesthetic to produce unconsciousness. Side-effects besides memory loss include headache, dizziness, muscle ache, nausea and vomiting, fear, panic, confusion, and physical weakness. The usual course of treatments is between 5 and 15, but up to 1000 shock treatments have been known to be given.

As regards the *experience* of shock treatment, patients' testimonies have described it as a form of torture that "made hell look like a health spa."

Lately, neurologist John Friedberg and others have been collecting extensive documentation to show that not only does shock treatment cause permanent, irreversible brain damge, but that there's no proof that it even works.

The greatest benefits derived from shock treatment are the financial ones going to the psychiatrist. Anyone planning to undertake psychotherapy should find out beforehand whether the prospective therapist uses shock treatment and avoid contact with all "shock doctors".

Fine, Paula. "Women and shock treatment." *Issues in Radical Therapy* 2(2) (1974): 9-11. (Back issues available for $1.00 from: IRT, Box 2324, Oakland, Ca. 94623, U.S.A.)

Frank, Leonard Roy. *The history of shock treatment.* Revised and expanded edition. San Francisco: Network Against Psychiatric Assault, 1978.

Now expanded to 206 pages. Contains more than 250 chronologically arranged excerpts and articles by opponents and proponents of electroshock. Includes a survey of 384 electroconvulsive treatment-related deaths, *MNN*'s

"Shock Doctor Roster", a 30-page glossary of psychiatric terms, an extensive bibliography and indexes. Illustrated. Available for $7 (California residents add 45¢ sales tax) from: Leonard Frank, 2300 Webster Street, San Francisco, Ca. 94115, U.S.A.

The Frank Papers. *Madness Network News* 2(5), December 1974.

This record of Leonard Frank's institutionalization is probably the most complete existing published record of a psychiatric hospitalization. It exposes the tyranny of psychiatrists and shock treatment.

Friedberg, John. *Shock treatment is not good for your brain*. San Francisco: Glide Publications, 1976.

Important recent document. Friedberg, a neurologist, challenges the psychiatric myth. Covers both electroconvulsive and insulin shock. Based on interviews with shock victims. Includes "The Frank Papers".

Friedberg. John. *Electro-convulsive therapy*. Article. March 20, 1975. Copies available from: Mental Patients Association, 2146 Yew Street, Vancouver V6K 3G7, British Columbia, CANADA.

Friedberg, John. "Electroshock therapy: let's stop blasting the brain." *Psychology Today* 9(3), August 1975.

"Shock treatments can damage brains and wipe out memories. What's more, there's no proof that they work."

Hudson, Wade. "Shock Treatment Testimony." *S.F.M.H.A.B. Inquiry*, January 20, 1974.

An article written by San Francisco Network Against Psychiatric Assault member. Copies available from: Mental Patients Association, 2146 Yew St., Vancouver V6K 3G7, B.C. CANADA.

Jones, Syl. "Electroshock opposed on clinical and constitutional grounds." *Modern Medicine*, February 15, 1975.

Laing, R.D. *The facts of life: an essay in feelings, facts, and phantasy*. New York: Random House/Pantheon, 1976.

Contains a number of Laing's personal observations of shock atrocities in hospitals where he has been; includes historical essay by shock pioneer, Ugo Cerletti. Relates story of successful concert violinist who, becoming depressed after a big tour, was given shock to "brighten her up" and suffered the side-effect of forgetting her violin repertoire forever.

Shock Doctor Roster. *Madness Network News*.

"Many psychiatric facilities, where shock treatment is administered, prepare 'shock rosters' naming those persons scheduled to be shocked at a given time. The MNN Shock Doctor Roster is made up of psychiatrists who administer or authorize shock treatment and their institutional affiliations. Listed psychiatrists, who no longer use this procedure, may notify *MNN* to have their names removed from the roster. Readers, who know of shock doctors who are not on the roster, are invited to submit their names along with their institution affiliation (city and state)." (from *MNN*, Oct. 1976) The last complete roster, listing 316 names, appeared in 4(6) Spring 1978. Henceforth, the complete roster will no longer appear on a regular basis, but will be printed on occasion.

Shock packet. Available from: Network Against Psychiatric Assault, 558 Capp Street, San Francisco, Ca. 94110, U.S.A.

Includes shock testimonies, Friedberg's "Let's Stop Blasting the Brain", and good shock bibliography.

Special Shock Issue. *In a Nutshell: Mental Patients Association Newsletter*, February, 1976.

Contains reports by MPA's Committee to Investigate Shock Treatment (Lawrence Belfrage and Kathy Kidd). The two main issues under scrutiny were alleged effectiveness and alleged safeness of shock treatment. Includes letters from shock patients, B.C. shock treatment statistics, and brief shock bibliography. Copies available from: Mental Patients Association, 2146 Yew St., Vancouver V6K 3G7 B.C. Canada.

Women Against Electric Shock Treatment. See VII-c, Women: Self-Help.

d) Drug Therapy

Today's most basic psychiatric tool is the mind-altering drug. This includes the major tranquilizers (Thorazine, Stelazine, Mellaril, Prolixin, etc.), the minor tranquilizers (Valium, Librium, Meprobamate, etc.), anti-depressants (Elavil, Tofranil, Parmate, etc.), an anti-manic-depressive (Lithium), sedatives (barbiturates, chloral hydrate, etc.), stimulants (Ritalin, Cylert, the Amphetamines), and others, including anti-Parkinsonian drugs (Cogentin, Tremin, etc.) to counter side-effects of the major tranquilizers.

The widespread use of psychoactive drugs began during the mid-fifties when the phenothiazine major tranquilizers were introduced into general usage among mental patient populations, being used to treat "schizophrenics" in particular. Most psychiatric drugs are "downers"; they have revolutionized psychiatric treatment by doping patients into a state of insensitivity and apathy.

All of these drugs produce undesirable side-effects and many are downright dangerous. Dry mouth, blurred vision, nausea, drowsiness, inability to concentrate, and uncontrollable muscle spasms are some common symptoms. The phenothiazines are among the most hazardous psychiatric drugs; they can produce a form of permanent brain damage known as *Tardive Dyskinesia.* Lithium, used to treat "manic-depressives", is another dangerous drug that can lead to poisoning.

Pharmaceutical companies, as the Sue Landers article explains, assume little responsibility for the patient using their drugs: information about their side-effects and hazards are tucked away in the fine-print section of drug ads which, because of the way the drugs are marketed and administered (often involuntarily), the patient never sees. Drug corporations, which annually reap the highest net profits in the U.S.A., put a lot more money into their high-pressure promoting to doctors than they do into research.

Mental patients liberation groups are working to make psychiatric drug information more readily available to consumers: in *Madness Network News,* Dr. Caligari's regular column presents detailed exposés on these drugs, their manufacturers, and abuses.

Since 1977, mental patients groups have organized a boycott of Smith, Kline, & French, the giant pharmaceutical firm that manufactures Thorazine, Stelazine, Parmate, and Eskalith. This company has been blatantly fighting the efforts of the Federal Drug Adminstration to regulate its overpricing and dangerous drugs, (see "The Politics of Phenothiazines"); it also has extensive interests in South Africa and other Third World countries. The organizers of the boycott are asking other groups and individuals to endorse their campaign against SK & F products, which also include Contac cold capsules, Sea & Ski products, Love Cosmetics, Sine-Off Nasal Spray, and Allergy Relief Medicine.

Anti-Forced Drugging Poster. See XI-c, Pamphlets, etc.

Briggs, David. *Consumer's guide to psychiatric medication.* Pamphlet. Newly revised and expanded, 1978. Available for $.50 (inmates and ex-inmates); or $1 (others) from Project Release (see Appendix B-a).

Produced entirely by ex-psychiatric inmates. Gives information on types, dosages, and side-effects of psychoactive drugs. Includes section on physical description of pills.

Caligari, Dr. *Madness Network News.* Regular column.

A licensed physician critically describes and discusses aspects of various psychiatric drugs, their current uses, politics, side-effects, etc.

Caligari, Dr. *Psychiatric drugs.* 24-page booklet. Newly revised and expanded, 1978. Available for $2.50 from Network Against Psychiatric Assault (see Appendix B-a).

"Very good information on the extremely destructive 'side-effects' of psychiatric drugs. Also good on the economics and politics of the drug industry." (Mad Librarian, *MNN* 3(6) 1976)

Do No Harm. Film. See XI-d, Audio-Visual.

Drug Ad Slides. See XI-d, Audio Visual

Fidell, Linda. *Put her down on drugs: prescribed usage in women.* KNOW No. 22604. Available for $ .40 from KNOW Inc. (See Appendix B-a)

Exposes medicine's sexist bias and willingness to dismiss women's complaints by drugging.

Goddard, James. "The medical business." *Scientific American*, Sept. 1973.

Hartman, Sylvia. "Princess Valium meets Shrink-Think." *The Radical Therapist* 1 (4) Nov., 1970. Also available in reprint as KNOW No. 09602 for $ .20 from KNOW Inc. (See Appendix B-a)

Another article that exposes medicine's sexist bias and willingness to dismiss women's complaints by drugging.

Harris, Bob. *A review of the literature and history of Lithium.* Available for $1.50 from Alliance for the Liberation of Mental Patients. (See Appendix B-a)

Landers, Sue. "Capitalism and the drug industry." *State and Mind* 5 (6) June-July, 1977.

Explores the drug industry's standing and function within the broader capitalist framework of business in America. Includes selected bibliography.

Lennard, Henry L. & Associates. *Mystification and drug abuse: hazards in using psychoactive drugs.* New York: Harper & Row/Perennial Library, 1972.

MPU dictionary of psychiatric drug side-effects. Available from 11 Acklam Road, London W10, England.

Comprehensive guide to the side-effects of psychiatric drugs ranging from Librium to Largactil. Based on both standard reference works and victims' personal statements. Explodes myths about these drugs' "beneficial" effects.

The politics of phenothiazines. Available for $1.50 from: Alliance for the Liberation of Mental Patients. (See Appendix B-a)

Contains information about Smith, Kline, and French (manufacturers of Thorazine, Stelazine, etc.) and the issue of forced drugging.

Sallychild, Andrea & Chandler, Dan. *The use and misuse of psychiatric drugs in California's mental health program.* Study. Available for $7.90 from Assembly Publications Office, Box 90, State Capital, Sacramento, Ca. 95814, USA.

This well-documented study done in 1977 combines science and politics. A good tool for activism against institutional psychiatry.

e) Behavior Mod

"Behavior mod" is a type of therapy where specific behaviors are changed by manipulating punishment and reward. It is a recent clinical outgrowth of the 20th century American Behaviorist School of psychology pioneered by John Watson and B.F. Skinner. The philosophy of behavioral psychologists hinges on the premise that in order to "shape" (i.e. control) behavior, it is not necessary to psychoanalyze the mind (consciousness, memories, the unconscious, etc.) but only to manipulate specific observable actions by "reinforcement" (i.e. reward or punishment).

This past decade has seen an alarming spread in behavior mod programs. The current favorite targets for this control method include prisoners, gays, and children. Behavior mod units are also becoming a fad. In prisons, punishment disguised as "treatment" is meted out under the name of *adverse therapy.* This includes painful electric shocks and drugs like Anectine which produce feelings similar to drowning. Sensory deprivation in solitary confinement is also used.

This section lists some writings that document these new behavior mod programs. See also IV-b, Prisons, VIII-c, Children, VIII-d, Gays and V-g, Mind Control: General & Misc.

Behaviour Mod Articles. *RT: A Journal of Radical Therapy* 4(1), 4(3), and 4(6), 1974. Copies available for $ .75 each from: RT Inc., P.O. Box 89, W. Somerville, Mass. 02144, U.S.A.

Chicago People's Law Office. "Check out your mind." *Rough Times*, 3(5), April-May, 1973.

Documents new wave of behaviour modification and psychosurgery in Federal and State Prisons. Also cites other articles in *RT* and elsewhere.

Common Sense. "Aversion therapy: straight at any price." *Rough Times* 3(4), 1973.

Describes some current practices of behaviour modification techniques designed for "curing" homosexuals.

Prisoners' letters on behaviour modification. *Rough Times* 3(5), 1973.

Documents some of the oppressive tactics used by prison officials to control prisoners' behaviour.

f) Psychological Testing

Psychological tests, another outgrowth of 20th century psychology, are presently used for a multitude of purposes. From "diagnosing" mental illness to "screening" docile workers and schoolchildren to "proving" the mental inferiority of blacks, these tests all give an aura of scientific respectability to the oppression of large groups of people.

The psychological testing industry, as Gross's *The Brain Watchers* documents, is a big business in itself. One of its most important functions is to define "normalcy" (i.e. what roles are allowed people). Another important function is to track down would-be deviants from this "normalcy" by applying its numerous screening and labelling techniques.

The following references explore the wide ramifications of psychological testing in such areas as class oppression, sexism, mentalism, racism, industry, and child control.

Baritz, Loren. *The servants of power*. Middletown, Conn.: Wesleyan University Press, 1960.

Surveys applied social science in industry.

Bickley, Richard. "Race, class and the I.Q. controversy." In *Rough times*, ed. by J. Agel. New York: Ballantine, 1973.

"In a society which is racist we should not be surprised that there would be theoreticians whose job it is to 'prove' the inferiority of the oppressed."

Block, N.J. and Dworkin, Gerald, eds. *The I.Q. controversy: critical readings*. See XI-b, Anthologies.

Brown, Phil. *Toward a marxist psychology*. New York: Harper & Row, 1974. Chapter 2: The Medical Model.

Discusses the transition from witch hunt practices (e.g. the test by "swimming") to modern methods of psychodiagnosis. Cites Szasz and others. (For more on Brown's book, see XI-a, Anti-Psychiatry, General Works.)

Friedman, Neil. *The social nature of psychological research: the psychological experiment as a social interaction*. New York: Basic Books, 1967.

Gross, Martin L. *The brain watchers*. New York: New American Library/ Signet, 1963.

A critical analysis of the multimillion-dollar psychological testing industry, this book attacks its frequently shoddy operations.

Kamin, Leon J. *The science and politics of I.Q.* Middlesex: Penguin, 1977.

Written by a sociologist, this academic study examines the classical data of I.Q. studies. It dismantles the theory that I.Q. is largely inherited, showing how the I.Q. test has historically served as an instrument of oppression and is a political rather than scientific tool.

Schrag, Peter and Divoky, Diane. *The myth of the hyperactive child: and other means of child control*. Chapter 4: Screening for Deviance and Other Diseases. (See also listing in VIII-c, Children)

Weisstein, Naomi. "Psychology constructs the female." See VII-a, Women: General Works.

g) Mind Control: General and Misc.

Behavior Control Newsletter. See XI-e, Periodicals.

Bibliography on behavior modification. 40 pages. Available for $3 from: Carleen Arlidge, 505 Alcatraz Ave., No. 15, Oakland, Ca. 94609, USA.

Compiled by radical criminology students. Includes references on all aspects of mind control.

Chorover, Stephan L. "Big brother and psychotechnology II: the pacification of the brain." *Psychology Today*, May 1974.

Ewen, Stuart. *Captains of consciousness: advertising and the social roots of the consumer culture.* New York: McGraw-Hill, 1976.

Provides a social history of the advertising industry and consumerism.

Federal Prisoners Coalition. "Brainwashing U.S. Prisoners." See IV-b, Prisons.

Good Times/Liberation News Service. "Vacaville: lobotomies, shock therapy, and torture for 'violent' California prisoners." See IV-b, Prisons.

"Human experimentation, psychiatry, and the press." Editorial. (Written by Tanya Temkin and arising out of collective discussion by the *Madness* staff) *Madness Network News* 4 (5) Winter, 1978.

Discusses mind-control experiments sponsored by the CIA and the hypocrisy of American psychiatrists who "hurl stones at Soviet psychiatry".

Key, Wilson Bryan. *Media sexploitation.* New York: New American Library/ Signet, 1976.

A study of consumer manipulation by the mass media.

Landerson, Louis/Liberation News Service. "Psychiatry and homosexuality: new 'cures'." See VIII-d, Gays.

Liberation News Service. "Electronic brain control." *Rough Times* 3(5),1973.

Describes some recent advances in electronic brain control and some of its proposed uses and implications.

McConnell, James V. "Criminals can be brainwashed—now." *Psychology Today* 3(11), April, 1970. (Also reprinted in R. Buckhout, et. al., eds. *Toward social change: a handbook for those who will.* New York: Harper & Row, 1971)

Mitford, Jessica. *Kind and unusual punishment.* See IV-b, Prisons.

Packard, Vance. *The hidden persuaders.* New York: Pocket Books, 1958.

This study, which was a No. 1 best seller, explores the operations of a modern-day branch of merchandising referred to as "motivation research". It documents how the techniques of psychiatry and the social sciences are being developed and used as a means to manipulate the unwary consumer.

Pines, Maya. *The brain changers, scientists and the new mind control.* New York: Harcourt Brace Jovanovich, 1973.

A journalistic survey of modern psychotechnology which includes a report and discussion of some of its abuses.

Prisoners describe mind control programmes. *Rough Times* 3(8), 1973.

A series of letters to *RT* documenting some prisoners' observations.

Ratner, Carl. "Radical psychology versus behaviourism." *Rough Times* 3 (8) 1973.

This article gives some of the theoretical bases of behaviourism, and shows how behaviourism is totally at odds with radical psychology.

Schrag, Peter. *Mind control.* New York: Pantheon Books, 1978.

A critical and well-documented report on the mind-control technology now being developed and used to control people.

Schrank, Jeffrey. *Snap, crackle and popular taste: the illusion of free choice in America.* New York: Delta, 1977.

A study of how advertising and the mass media are used for purposes of social control, while creating the illusion of freedom through "pseudo-choices".

Seem, Mark & Parkin, John. " 'Mental health' normalization and resistance." *State and Mind* 6 (1) Fall, 1977.

Discusses the growing power of psychiatry and its "technology of normalization". Argues that these "soft" techniques of intervention are potentially just as menacing as the "hard" psychiatric techniques (psychosurgery etc.).

VI. Professionalism
and
the Mental Health Industry

VI PROFESSIONALISM AND THE MENTAL HEALTH INDUSTRY

Writings in this section critically examine the inner workings of the psychiatric empire: how it functions in capitalist society; how "mental health" operates as a big business enterprise; how the mystique of professionalism gives psychiatrists the power to create a monopoly on expertise; and how psychiatry uses its power to act as an agent for social control.

As members of a professional class, psychiatrists enjoy all the benefits and protection usually given that social position. They are regarded (and regard themselves) as the ultimate authorities on mental health. This authority gives them the power to define who is mad and who is sane.

To maintain their authority, psychiatrists surround their work with the trappings that traditionally serve to isolate and empower a group: they speak a specialized jargon; claim to be neutral and objective; charge outrageous fees; accept regulation and criticism only from their own kind, scorning advice from the masses they "serve"; guard their territory jealously, attacking any rival ideologies; demand years of expensive, isolated training before anyone can join their ranks; and exercise power over an entire hierarchy of subordinate mental health workers.

Psychiatry is far from neutral. Shrinks generally come from middle or upper class backgrounds; their training thoroughly reinforces ruling class values, and they in turn become one of their class' main enforcers.

The writings listed here represent a fairly broad range of perspectives. They go all the way from varied critiques of the psychiatric profession by regular shrinks, "radical therapists" and other professionals to Marxist-type analyses (and/or condemnations) of the entire mental health system. Further writings which expose the economics and politics of the mental health industry are listed in V-d, Drug Therapy and V-f, Psychological Testing.

Adams, Joe K. "Violence and 'schizophrenia'." *Madness Network News* 2(1), 1974.

Exposes some facts behind the myths perpetuated about mental patients.

Beckman, Lanny. "Psychology as a social problem: an investigation into the Society for the Psychological Study of Social Issues (SPSSI)." In *Rough times,* ed. by J. Agel. New York: Ballantine, 1973.

A condemnation of psychology in general and the SPSSI in particular. Attacks irrelevancy of psychology, how it serves the capitalist/imperialist system, its uselessness to help solve the problems it allegedly studies, and how its practitioners only get richer.

Beckman, Lanny and Persky, Stan. "On the political and economic implications of Canadian psychiatry." *M.P.A. Research Section*, January 1974.

Examines the typical response of the Canadian mental health industry to a threatened encroachment on its empire by the Human Potential Movement. Exposes the essentially economic nature of Canadian psychiatry. Available for $1 from: Vancouver Mental Patients Association (see Appendix B-a for address).

Benziger, Barbara Field. *Speaking out: doctors and patients on emotional health*. New York: Walker & Co., 1976.

This uncritical survey covers every type of therapy. Contains short section on Mental Patients Liberation Project.

Braginsky, D.D. and Braginsky, B.M. "Psychologists: high priests of the middle class." *Psychology Today* 7(7) (December 1973): 15-20, 138.

Brandt, Anthony. *Reality police: the experience of insanity in America.* New York: William Morrow and Co., 1975.

Written by a journalist who signed himself in and was soon denied his individual interests by the institution. Pokes holes in the psychiatric model.

Brown, Phil. *Towards a Marxist psychology.* New York: Harper & Row, 1974.

This exploratory work examines relationships between class structure, capitalism and the mental health industry. Brown was trained as a psychologist and worked as an early member of the RT Collective. Also see IX-a, Anti-Psychiatry, General Works.

Chu, Franklin and Trotter, Sharland. *The madness establishment: Ralph Nader's Study Group Report on the National Institute of Mental Health*. New York: Grossman Publishers, 1974.

Report from a Nader Group study of community mental health centers. Its results are revealing, but the report fails to go far enough or to question the medical model.

Clark, Ted. "The mythology of professionalism and an emerging alternate role." In *In search of a therapy: personal accounts of the training, change and growth of nonconventional therapists,* ed. by D. Jaffe. New York: Harper & Row, 1975.

Cousens, Ken. "Professionalism: Reply to Henley and Brown." In *Rough times*, ed. by J. Agel. New York: Ballantine, 1973.

Attacks radical intellectual perspective based on theory and "shoulds" rather than on social practice. Says that skills are not a myth, but that they come from practice and their demystification occurs as they become more accessible to the people.

Dubreuil, Guy and Wittkower, Eric D. "Psychiatric anthropology: a historical persepective." *Psychiatry*, 39(2) (May 1976): 130-41.

Gives brief overview of psychiatric anthropology as a discipline. Traces common ideological origins of psychiatrist and anthropologist, both of whom engage in the study and classification of "misfits" in western capitalist/

imperialist culture. Argues how convergence of these two disciplines becomes a logical development.

Glenn, Michael L. "On professionalism." In *Rough times*, ed. by J. Agel. New York: Ballantine, 1973.

Addresses professionals on how they can be radical therapists and help change the status quo.

Glenn, Michael and Kunnes, Richard. *Repression or revolution? therapy in the United States today*. New York: Harper & Row, 1973.

Exposes the social control function of psychotherapy and how it serves the status quo.

Gordon, James S. "Psychiatric miseducation." In *In search of a therapy: personal accounts of the training, change, and growth of nonconventional therapists*, ed. by D. Jaffe. New York: Harper& Row, 1975.

Halleck, Seymour L. *The politics of therapy*. New York: Harper & Row, 1972.

Halleck, a psychiatrist, argues that members of his profession have a moral obligation to examine the social consequences of their practices. He offers a philosophical and ethical framework to provide guidelines for psychiatric intervention, but his own political consciousness seems to get a bit wishy-washy.

Henley, Nancy and Brown, Phil. "The myth of skill and the class nature of professionalism." In *Rough times*, ed. by J. Agel. New York: Ballantine, 1973

Exposes the class nature of the mental health system.

Jaffe, Dennis T. "The healer, the community, or the bureaucrat." In *In search of a therapy: personal accounts of the training, change, and growth of nonconventional therapists*, ed. by Dennis T. Jaffe. New York: Harper & Row, 1975.

Keniston, Kenneth. "How community mental health stamped out the riots, 1968-78." *Transaction* 5(8) (1968): 21-9.

A parody on psychiatric fascism.

Kunnes, Richard. *Your money or your life: Rx for the medical market place.* New York: Dodd, Mead & Co., 1971.

Exposes the American health care system and the medical-industrial complex.

Kunnes, Rick. "Detherapizing society." In *Rough times*, ed. by J. Agel. New York: Ballantine, 1973.

Margaro, Peter A., Oripp, Robert & McDowell, David J. *The mental health industry: a cultural phenomenon.* New York: John Wiley & Sons, 1978.

Three psychologists write an academic style critique of mental health professionals.

Mead, M. "Some relationships between social anthropology and psychiatry." In *Dynamic psychiatry*, ed. by F. Alexander and H. Rose. Chicago: University of Chicago Press, 1952.

"Psychiatry as social control – a political analysis." *Madness Network News,* 4(2) Spring, 1977.

"Psychiatry is inherently oppressive. It will accommodate to the power relations of the society in which it is located. Psychiatry is not a field of healing, but of social control. The 'mental health' system is an industry that produces physical illness and emotional misery, not health. We do not believe that the oppressiveness of the mental illness system can be combatted in and of itself, isolated from other oppressive systems in this country. The mental illness system supports and is supported by the institutions of racism, sexism, classism, ageism, and capitalism. Therefore, we believe that the mental illness system will only be overthrown as the institutions of racism, sexism, classism, ageism and capitalism are overthrown. The mental illness system is one of the main tools of mind control (along with schools, the media, etc.) used to keep us divided, fearful of ourselves and each other, and identifying with the interests of the ruling class." This excellent analysis, written in various stages by several members of the MPLF in Boston and NAPA in San Francisco (although not yet endorsed by either group), goes on to outline the oppression of the "mental illness system" through the institutions mentioned.

Statman, Jim. "Community mental health as a pacification program." In *The radical therapist,* ed. by J. Agel. New York: Ballantine, 1971.

Examines political and social functions of community mental health programs in urban ghettos.

Taylor, R.L. and Torrey, E.F. "The pseudoregulation of American psychiatry." *American Journal of Psychiatry* 129(6) (1972): 658-62.

Torrey, E. Fuller. *The mind game: witchdoctors and psychiatrists*. New York: Bantam, 1973.

Torrey, a psychiatrist, systematically undermines the assumptions used to justify psychiatric chauvinism and imperialism. Providing a framework for understanding the activities of psychotherapists around the world, he argues for the validity of "witchdoctors" and their practices. Valuable sourcebook of comprehensively documented proof that the psychiatric establishment's monopoly on "mental healing" is unjustified.

Torrey, E. Fuller. *The death of psychiatry*. Baltimore: Penguin, 1975.

Based upon a solid Szaszian foundation, this book takes the practice of psychiatry through total demolition of the medical model and beyond, into an alternative educational model where problems in living become the province of "tutors". In Chapter 10, "Problems of Living versus Brain Disease: 'Schizophrenia' Revisited", Torrey takes a good step forward in clarifying the muddled question of true "mental disease"; points out how diagnostic tests for organic brain disease are improving and could be made more accessible, and that the small minority of *proven* cases should be given back to neurology.

Webbink, Pat. "Therapist turned woman." In *Rough times*, ed. by J. Agel. New York: Ballantine, 1973.

Webbink, a therapist, goes to an American Psychological Association convention and has her eyes opened at this carnival of ego-trippers.

Weitz, Don. "Mental health oppression: Canadian style." *Rough Times* 3(7), 1973. (Back issues available for $ .50 each from: RT, Inc., P.O. Box 89, W. Somerville, Mass. 02144 U.S.A.)

Exposes the mental health industry in Canada, particularly Ontario.

VII. Psychiatry and
Women

VII PSYCHIATRY AND WOMEN

Today, the psychiatric system is a key instrument for the oppression of women. Beginning with Freud's theories of sexuality, psychiatry has always advanced the stereotype of women as passive and dependent; any woman who doesn't fit this role can be labelled "mentally ill" and in need of psychiatric treatment.

Psychiatric treatment, in its many forms, is a lucrative practice which exploits women as consumers of the profit-oriented mental health industries. The type of treatment a woman receives is generally divided along class lines: women from higher socio-economic strata receive private psychotherapy or analysis, while poor women are usually incarcerated in mental institutions where personal attention from a psychiatrist is replaced by drugs and electroshock.

Since around 1970, a large number of writings attacking the psychiatric oppression of women has appeared. While much of the mainstream anti-psychiatry literature (e.g. British Anti-Psychiatry and Thomas Szasz), has not dealt with sexism in psychiatry, many feminists and mental patients liberation activists have been producing a wealth of resource materials. In addition to these writings, a new type of counselling — feminist therapy — has emerged as a non-sexist alternative to traditional therapy.

Writings in this section examine women's position in the mental health system from many angles: writers such as Ehrenrich and English provide a history of the sexist foundations of medicine/psychiatry; Phyllis Chesler's classic, *Women and Madness,* explores in detail women's careers as mental patients and shows how psychiatry keeps women powerless and locked into male-defined sex roles.

a) General Works

Studies in the psychiatric oppression of women; the truth behind myths that psychiatry has perpetuated about women; writings toward a feminist psychology of women; other relevant works of feminist analysis.

Bardwick, Judith. *The psychology of women: a bio-cultural conflict*. New York: Harper & Row, 1971.

A classic work on the psychology of women.

Bart, Pauline B. "The myth of a value-free psychotherapy." in *Towards social change: a handbook for those who will*, ed. by R. Buckhout et. al. New York: Harper & Row, 1971.

Bart, a sociologist, is the author of numerous studies on the sociology of psychiatry. This work examines therapy from a feminist perspective. Copies also available for 75¢ from: Dr. Pauline Bart, Dept. of Psychiatry, University of Illinois Medical School, Chicago, Illinois, U.S.A.

Bart, Pauline, B. "Depression in middle-aged women ('Portnoy's Mother's Complaint') In *Woman in sexist society: studies in power and powerlessness*, ed. by V. Gornick and B. Moran. New York: New American Library /Signet. 1972.

Beam, Joanna. "Sexism in psychiatry." *Issues in Radical Therapy* 1(4), October 1973.

Beam, Joanna. "Sexism in psychosurgery." Article reprint included in *LAMP Information Packet*. See XI-c, Pamphlets.

Boston Lesbian Feminists. "Vietnam: a feminist analysis." In *Rough times*, ed. by J. Agel. New York: Ballantine, 1973.

Discusses the politics of rape and the rapist mentality.

Chamberlin, Judi. "Women's oppression and psychiatric oppression." In *Women look at psychiatry*, ed. by D. Smith and S. David. Vancouver: Press Gang Publishers, 1975.

This essay by mental patients' liberation activist raises an important and necessary issue: that "...anti-psychiatric writers (both feminist and others) continue to perpetuate the stereotype that someone else must speak for the mental patient". Chamberlin develops argument to illustrate necessity for analysis of psychiatric oppression to be made by mental patients.

Chesler, Phyllis. "Marriage and psychotherapy." In *The radical therapist*, ed. by J. Agel. New York: Ballantine, 1971.

Outlines similar basis for women entering both marriage and psychotherapy, the two major socially approved institutions for women. Also available as No. 08201 for $ .10 from: KNOW Inc., P.O. Box 86031, Pittsburgh, Pennsylvania 15221 U.S.A.

Chesler, Phyllis. "Men drive women crazy." *Psychology Today* 5(2), July 1971

Chesler, Phyllis. "Patient and patriarch: women in the psychotherapeutic relationship." In *Woman in sexist society: studies in power and powerlessness*, ed. by V. Gornick and B. Moran. New York: New American Library /Signet, 1972.

Facts about women as psychotherapy patients in America: their "symptoms"; why there are more women involved with mental health professionals than there are men; who the therapists are and their views about women; practical implications for women in a psychotherapeutic relationship.

Chesler, Phyllis. *Women and madness*. New York: Avon Books, 1973.

Chesler's monumental document explores the realities behind women's careers as psychiatric patients. It clarifies how, for women, the treadmill of mental illness/psychotherapy is driven by sex role stereotyping. Exposes the violence that psychiatry perpetuates against all women.

Chesler, Phyllis & Goodman, Emily Jane. *Women, money & power.* New York: Bantam, 1977.

An analysis of the current North American capitalist economic system as it relates to women, this book explodes the myth of women having financial power. It also explores the possibilities of women gaining access to the financial machinery of capitalism as a starting point to change society. "Without an understanding of money and power and institutions, women can never be prepared for capitalism or its *successor*." The book's weakness lies in the fact that it doesn't propose alternatives to capitalism in which equal division of that power would end women's exploitation.

Chesler, Phyllis and Richmond Coll., City U., New York. "A word about mental health and women." *Mental Hygiene* 57(3) (Summer 1973): 5-7.

Committee for the Defense of Soviet Political Prisoners. *Women political prisoners in the U.S.S.R.* Pamphlet. New York: CDSPP Press, 1975. Available from: P.O. Box 142, Cooper Station, New York, N.Y. 10003, U.S.A.

Cox, Sue (ed.) *Female psychology: the emerging self*. See XI-b, Anthologies.

Ehrenreich, Barbara and English, Deirdre. *Complaints and disorders: the sexual politics of sickness.* Old Westbury, N.Y.: The Feminist Press/ Glass Mountain Pamphlet (No. 2), 1973.

Feminist study of history of the medical system, illustrated. Shows how early medical ideology found its culmination in a new "female disease" called hysteria, which in turn allowed Freud and his followers to create the medical speciality of psychiatry. Available from: The Feminist Press, SUNY/ College at Old Westbury, Box 334, Old Westbury, New York 11568, U.S.A.

Feminist Studies Program. *Women and psychology*. Bibliography.

Guide to twentieth century literature on women and psychology. Contains both popular and scientific writings. Available for $ .50 from: Feminist Studies Program, Cambridge-Goddard Graduate School, 5 Upland Road, Cambridge, Mass. 02140, U.S.A.

Figes, Eva. *Patriarchal Attitudes*. London: Virago, 1978.

Theoretical work examining, among other things, the role of Freudian psychoanalysis in the oppression of women.

Fine, Paula. "Women and shock treatment." *Issues in Radical Therapy* 2(2) (1974): 9-11.

Firestone, Shulamith. *The dialectic of sex: the case for feminist revolution*. New York: Bantam, 1971.

Classic manifesto of radical feminist ideology. Postulates that dualism of Otherness originates from sexual division. Includes chapter on "Freudianism: The Misguided Feminism."

Frankfort, Ellen. *Vaginal politics.* New York: Bantam, 1973.

"About the struggle of women with contemporary health care in this country." Examines relationship between women patients and their male physicians. Discusses abortion, drugs, cancer, V.D., and other topics. Includes sections on psychiatrists, feminist therapy, and mental patients' liberation.

Garskoff, Michele H., ed. *Roles women play: readings towards women's liberation.* See XI-b, Anthologies.

Gornick, Vivian and Moran, Barbara K., eds. *Woman in sexist society: studies in power and powerlessness*. See XI-b, Anthologies.

Horney, Karen. *Feminine psychology*. Edited with Introduction by Harold Kelman. New York: W.W. Norton, 1967.

Pioneer classic by well-known woman analyst; criticizes Freud's theories of female psychosexual development. Argues that what woman really envies is not man's penis but masculine attributes and the opportunities society offers more readily to men.

Huber, Joan, ed. *Changing women in a changing society*. See XI-b, Anthologies.

Koedt, Anne. "The myth of the vaginal orgasm." in *The radical therapist*, ed. by J. Agel. New York: Ballantine, 1971.

Explodes sexual myths perpetuated about women by male psychiatrists and other men for the purpose of maintaining the sexual status quo (at women's expense).

Lerner, Judy. "Women and involuntary hospitalization." Article reprint included in *LAMP Information Packet*. See XI-c, Pamphlets.

Maccoby, Eleanor E. and Jacklin, Carol N. *The psychology of sex differences*. Stanford, Ca.: Stanford University Press, 1974.

Comprehensive review of research on sex differences—hormonal, genetic,social. Contains extensive bibliography.

Miller, Jean Baker, ed. *Psychoanalysis and women.* See XI-b, Anthologies.

Martin, Del. *Battered wives*. San Francisco: Glide Publications, 1976.

First major report to be published on this form of violence. Points out how professionals (including mental health professionals) have ignored this problem; shows failures of legal system and social services. Contains survival tactics, legislative proposals, refuge resources for battered women.

Millman, Marcia and Kanter, Rosabeth Moss, eds. *Another voice: feminist perspectives on social life and social science.* See XI-b, Anthologies.

Millett, Kate. *Sexual politics*. New York: Doubleday, 1970.

Important feminist classic.

Mitchell, Juliet. *Psychoanalysis and feminism: Freud, Reich, Laing, and women.* New York: Random House/Vintage, 1975.

Argues that "a rejection of psychoanalysis and of Freud's work is fatal for feminism. However it may have been used, psychoanalysis is not a recommendation *for* a patriarchal society, but an analysis *of* one." Mitchell believes that Freud has ultimately more to offer women's liberation than Reich or Laing. She also examines writings of neo-feminists (de Beauvoir, Friedan, Figes, Greer, Firestone, Millett), attacking them for their rejection of Freud.

Morgan, Robin, ed. *Sisterhood is powerful*. See XI-b, Anthologies.

Packard, Elizabeth P. Ware. *Modern persecution; or insane asylums unveiled*. See IV-a, Psychiatry and Institutions: Mental Hospitals.

Packard, Elizabeth P. Ware. *Great disclosure of spiritual wickedness in high places: with appeal to the government to protect the inalienable rights of women.* (Reprinted from 1865 edition) New York: Arno Press, 1974.

Packard, Elizabeth P. Ware. "Madness and marriage." in *The age of madness: the history of involuntary mental hospitalization presented in selected texts*, ed. by T.S. Szasz. Garden City, New York: Doubleday/Anchor, 1973.

Documents how Packard, because she wouldn't submit to her husband's religious opinions, was declared insane and locked away. Gives proceedings of her subsequent fight to secure her freedom.

Quinn, Alice. "Insanity and control: a class trap." *Quest: A Feminist Quarterly* 1(3). Back issues available from: *Quest*, P.O. Box 8843, Washington, D.C., 20003, U.S.A.

"Analysis of the classist, sexist, and heterosexist assumptions of psychiatric theory and practice, by a working-class lesbian ex-inmate. Quinn criticizes 'feminist therapy' and other alternative therapies as being classist rip-offs which deny the reality of working-class and psychiatric inmates' oppression." (Mad Librarian, *Madness Network News,* 4(6) 1978).

A Redstockings Sister. "Brainwashing and women." In *The radical therapist*, ed. by J. Agel. New York: Ballantine, 1971.

Smith, Dorothy E. and David, Sara J., eds. *Women look at psychiatry*. See XI-b, Anthologies.

Special Issue: "Women and mental health." *Chomo-Uri*. See I-c, Mental Patient Experience: Other Misc. Literature.

Tennov, Dorothy. *Psychotherapy: the hazardous cure*. Garden City, New York: Doubleday/Anchor, 1976.

Critical study of psychotherapy by feminist consulting psychologist. Gives comprehensive discussion of dangers of psychotherapy, especially as it relates to women.

Walstedt, Joyce. *36-24-36, Anatomy of oppression: a feminist analysis of psychotherapy*. KNOW No. 17205.

Exposes sexist biases of psychoanalytical theories of women and presents feminist therapy alternatives. Available for $ .50 from: KNOW Inc., P.O. Box 86031, Pittsburgh, Pennsylvania 15221 U.S.A.

Walstedt, Joyce Jennings. *The psychology of women: a partially annotated bibliography*.

Comprehensive book-length listing of psychological literature on psychology of women. Main focus is on professional research journal articles. Available for $2.00 plus .25 postage from: KNOW Inc., P.O. Box 86031, Pittsburg, Pennsylvania 15221 U.S.A.

Weisstein, Naomi. "Psychology constructs the female." In *Woman in sexist society: studies in power and powerlessness*, ed. by V. Gornick and B. Moran. New York: New American Library/Signet, 1972.

Discusses psychology's sexist assumptions (but actual ignorance) about women and how its theories serve to perpetuate this ignorance. Weisstein, a psychologist, has also written numerous other papers on a variety of subjects, including sex differences.

"Women and psychology" issue. *The Radical Therapist* 3(1), 1971.

Special *RT* issue devoted to women. Edited by Judith Brown.

"Women's Issue". *RT: A Journal of Radical Therapy* 4(5), 1974.

Includes articles on anger, rape, woman as healer, heterosexual politics, women and psychology, plus resource list.

Women locked up. Special issue of *Women, a Journal of Liberation.* 3(3). See IV-b, Prisons.

b) Lesbians

Until early this decade, lesbian literature was pretty much monopolized by either male psychiatrists peddling the Freudian dogma of lesbianism as "disease", or by literary moralizers weaving melodramas of the tragic lesbian. (Not to mention the mountains of pulp pornography—pseudo-realist exposes of "lesbians at play"—invented and written by men for the entertainment of other men.) Psychiatrists had become the self-appointed spokesmen for the lesbian: she thus found herself officially defined in our society as "sick". Now great numbers of lesbians are writing the truth about themselves; at present, their analysis of psychiatric (and other oppressions) of lesbians tends to come more from a feminist rather than a gay liberation perspective. See also VIII-d, Gays, for further material relevant to gay oppression and liberation.

Abbott, Sidney and Love, Barbara. *Sappho was a right-on woman: a liberated view of lesbianism*. New York: Stein & Day, 1972.

Pioneer work relating lesbianism to feminism. Tells what it was like to come out during pre-feminist times; continues on into early days of lesbian activism in women's movement; then beyond, to a vision of the future, where lesbians can operate openly as whole people.

Grahn, Judy. *Edward the Dyke*. Oakland: Women's Press Collective, 1971.

Prose/poem about how the straight psychiatric institution tries to turn Edward the dyke into a "normal healthy heterosexual woman".

Johnston, Jill. *Lesbian nation: the feminist solution*. New York: Simon & Schuster/Touchstone, 1973.

Personal statement by well-known lesbian author and columnist who was also once an incarcerated "schizophrenic". Certain portions of this book appeared in earlier form in *The Village Voice.*

Long Time Coming Collective. *The myth of madness*. Pamphlet.

Lesbians writing about their experiences with psychiatrists and mental hospitals; interviews with lesbians in mental health professions; stories; poetry; and information. Available for $1.25 from: Long Time Coming, Box 161, Station E, Montreal H2T 3A7, Quebec, CANADA.

Martin, Del and Lyon, Phyllis. *Lesbian/Woman*. San Francisco: Glide Publications, 1972.

Modern lesbian classic explores situation of lesbian as woman from a feminist viewpoint. Martin and Lyon were founding members of the Daughters of Bilitis, oldest and largest all-female homophile organization in the U.S., and also edited its journal, *The Ladder*.

Radicalesbians. "The woman identified woman." In *Radical psychology*, ed. by P. Brown. New York: Harper & Row, 1973.

Basic lesbian document, which begins: "What is a lesbian? A lesbian is the rage of all women condensed to the point of explosion."

Rule, Jane. *Lesbian images*. New York: Pocket Books/Simon & Schuster, 1976.

Rule gives a brief analysis of being a lesbian writer and its implications and goes on to talk about some of the more famous of them including Willa Cather, Radclyffe Hall, May Sarton, Gerturde Stein, Violette le Duc, Vita Sackville-West and Ivy Compton Burnett. A brief chapter at the end discusses more current lesbian non-fiction. Includes short bibliography of lesbian fiction and non-fiction.

RT: A Journal of Radical Therapy 4(8), 1974.

This issue contains articles on lesbians in therapy.

Shelley, Martha. "Lesbianism." In *The radical therapist*, ed. by J. Agel. New York: Ballantine, 1971.

Basic lesbian document, proclaims that: "If hostility to men causes lesbianism, then it seems to me that in a male-dominated society lesbianism is a sign of mental health."

c) Self-Help and Self-Defence Resources

Bateman, Py. "You can fight off a rapist and survive." *Black Belt* 15(8) August, 1977. Back issues available for $2 each from: Black Belt Magazine, 1845 W. Empire Ave., Burbank, Ca. 91504, U.S.A.

"Women are subject to various types of assaults, from purse-snatching, to rape, to murder," writes Bateman, and "every woman should think about it ahead of time and be prepared to react in some way." This valuable article by a woman karate black belt provides concise, practical information. It includes a feminist analysis of rape and some basic self-defense techniques. Bateman also stresses that women must stop carrying themselves timidly and fearfully but, rather, exude an air of self-confidence and determination not to brook any intrusion upon their person.

Boston Women's Health Collective. *Our bodies ourselves: a book by and for women*. New York: Simon & Schuster/Touchstone. 1973.

Covers nutrition, exercise, rape, self-defence, sexuality, V.D., birth control, abortion, childbearing, menopause, health care. Includes a Boston Gay collectives advice to lesbians on psychiatric treatment.

Cheda, Sherill. *The mind rapists*. KNOW, No. 24903.

An annotated bibliography for persons seeking help for mental pain. Available for $ .30 from: KNOW Inc., P.O. Box 86031, Pittsburgh, Pennsylvania 15221 U.S.A.

Clark, Lorenne and Lewis, Debra, eds. *Rape: the price of coercive sexuality.* Toronto: Women's Press, 1977.

Connell, Noreen and Wilson, Cassandra, eds. *Rape: the first sourcebook for women by New York Radical Feminists*. New York: New American Library/ Plume, 1974.

Discusses current attitudes of police courts and hospitals. Covers consciousness raising about the politics of rape; personal experiences of victims; child abuse; rape laws—current and proposed; how to organize rape protection groups; self-defense techniques; changing society's attitudes.

Cowan, Belita. *Women's health care: resources, writings, bibliographies.* 60 pages. Available for $4 with a 30% discount for anyone who can't afford it, from: Anshen Publishing Co., 556 Second Street, Ann Arbor, Mi. 48103, U.S.A.

Grimstad, Kirsten and Rennie, Susan. *The new woman's survival sourcebook*. New York: Alfred A. Knopf, 1975.

Documents the "ideas of feminism" with information about self-help, self-defence, health, spirituality, legal issues, etc. Outlines resources, books, journals, pamphlets, and organizations devoted to all major aspects of women's culture today. Includes excellent section on mental health resources for women.

Psychological karate: how to fight sexist therapy. Pamphlet. Available from: Anne Seiden, Institute for Juvenile Research, 1140 South Paulina, Chicago, Illinois, U.S.A.

Rape Crisis Booklets. Available from: Rape Crisis Centre, P.O. Box 20015, Washington, D.C. 20009 U.S.A.

1) *How to Start a Rape Crisis Centre*. Booklet. $1.25.
2) *Protection Tactics*. Pamphlet. Free upon receipt of self-addressed, stamped envelope.
3) *The Washington Centre's Bimonthly Newsletter* lists books, magazine articles, and studies of rape. Subscription $2.00.

Redstockings (San Francisco). "What you can do." In *The radical therapist*, ed. by J. Agel. New York: Ballantine, 1971.

Gives a list of suggestions to therapists about what they can do to stop oppressing women.

Women against electric shock treatment. Pamphlet.

Four women who have been involved with shock (two as patients; two as hospital workers) share their knowledge of how EST is currently used to brutalize women. Available for $ .35 from: Women Against Electric Shock Treatment, 5251 Broadway, Oakland, Ca. 94618 U.S.A. See also Appendix B-b, Directory: Women, *Women Against Electric Shock Treatment*.

d) Feminist Therapy

"Feminist therapy" is a broad term covering many sometimes contradictory practices. At its best, it can be women in consciousness-raising-type groups. working together to ease the pain of their oppression and finding ways to effect change within both their personal lives and society as a whole. At its worst, it can be the same old psychiatric oppression repackaged in a non-sexist wrapper.

The problem of defining what feminist therapy is, could, and should be is taken up by Karen Chase's article. Chase points out the contradictions a professional feminist therapist must face in her role of feminist on one hand, and as member of a hierarchical male-oriented profession on the other. Her article goes on to say that feminist therapy must become more responsible to the women's movement, a political rather than therapeutic strategy, and ultimately an instrument for the goals of women's liberation.

Some women have found feminist mental health professionals helpful to them (see Barbara Joyce's article). Other writers point out that despite sometimes good intentions, middle-class feminist shrinks are out of touch with the reality of their clients' lives and ultimately contribute to perpetuating mentalism (see articles by Chamberlin and Quinn in VII-a, General Works).

The writings by feminist therapists listed here reveal, despite ongoing controversies, a form of therapy that is an obvious improvement on conventional sexist therapy. Other more self-help-type feminist therapies, such as the de-professionalized services at Elizabeth Stone House and consciousness-raising groups (see Marilyn Zweig), are an important tool for women.

Chase, Karen. "Seeing sexism: a look at feminist therapy." *State and Mind* 5(5) March-April, 1977.

Discusses some problems of defining "feminist therapy".

David, Sara. "Becoming a non-sexist therapist." In *Women look at psychiatry*, ed. by D. Smith and S. David. Vancouver: Press Gang Publishers, 1975.

"Successful therapy with women requires a fundamental belief in their abilities to function well in all situations, and to take on and fulfill responsibilities in all the same areas as men with equal competence."

David. Sara. "Emotional self-defence groups for women." In *Women look at psychiatry*, ed. by D. Smith and S. David. Vancouver: Press Gang Publishers, 1975.

Describes David's work in women's groups at Simon Fraser University.

Ehrenreich, Barbara and English, Deirdre. *Witches, midwives and nurses: a history of women healers*. Old Westbury, New York: The Feminist Press/ Glass Mountain Pamphlet (No. 1), 1973.

Examines women's role in medicine, male control of the health industry, and the political suppression of female healers by the medical establishment. Illustrated. Available from: The Feminist Press, SUNY/College at Old Westbury, Box 334, Old Westbury, New York 11568, U.S.A.

Ehrenreich, Barbara, and English, Deirdre. *For her own good; 50 years of the experts' advice to women.* New York: Anchor Press/Doubleday, 1978.

"Elizabeth Stone House." In *The new woman's survival sourcebook,* ed. by K. Grimstad and S. Rennie. New York: Alfred A. Knopf, 1975.

About a pioneer feminist therapeutic community in the Boston area, why and how it began; how it currently operates to help women in crisis. Also see Appendix B-b, Directory: Women.

"Elizabeth Stone House." *RT: A Journal of Radical Therapy* 4(6) Spring 1975.

"Feminist Therapists' Conference." *Big Mama Rag* 4(3) March 1976.

Reports of the January 1976 feminist therapists' conference in Boulder, Colorado. Discusses conference's problems of professional elitism and resultant lack of solidarity among those wishing to participate.

Feminist Therapist Roster. Contact the national coordinator: Nechama Liss-Levinson, Department of Psychiatry, Lab Office Building 2313, SUNY, Stony Brook, N.Y. 11794 U.S.A.

The Association for Women in Psychology has compiled a list of feminist therapists and a roster of feminist therapist area coordinators to help people find feminist therapists. If you're looking for one in your area or you want to be listed, contact the national coordinator.

Feminist Therapy Bibliographies. Available for $1.00 each ($2.75/set) from: Womanspace Inc., 636 Beacon St., Boston, Mass. 02215 U.S.A.

1) *Counselling Women.*
2) *Issues in the Psychology and Counselling of Women*.
3) *Women: Sexuality, Psychology and Psychotherapy*.

Griffith, Alison. "Feminist counselling: a perspective." In *Women look at psychiatry*, ed. by D. Smith and S. David. Vancouver: Press Gang Publishers, 1975.

Discusses the role of feminist counselling in women's liberation.

Guidelines for women seeking psychotherapy. Pamphlet.

Written from feminist viewpoint. Describes types of therapists available and how to evaluate their services. Available for $.50 from: Cleveland Women's Counselling, P.O. Box 18472, Cleveland, Oh. 44118 U.S.A.

Hanisch, Carol. "The personal is political." In *The radical therapist*, ed. by J. Agel. New York: Ballantine, 1971. (First appeared in *Notes from the Second Year: Women's Liberation, Major Writings of the Radical Feminists*, ed. by S. Firestone and A. Koedt).

"One of the first things we discover in these groups is that personal problems are political problems. There are no personal solutions at this time. There is only collective action for a collective solution."

"How feminist is feminist therapy?" (A 3-part article) *Off Our Backs: A Women's News Journal.* Sept. 1976. Available for $.45 from Off Our Backs, 1724–20th St. N.W., Washingon D.C. 20002 U.S.A.

Joyce, Barbara. "I'm not crazy after all." In *Women look at psychiatry*, ed. by D. Smith and S. David. Vancouver: Press Gang Publishers, 1975.

Autobiographical account of a journey through the feminist therapy process.

MacDonald, Rita and Smith, Dorothy. "A feminist therapy session." In *Women look at psychiatry*, ed. by D. Smith and S. David. Vancouver: Press Gang Publishers, 1975.

Mander, Anica Vesel and Rush, Anne Kent. *Feminism as therapy*. New York: Random House/Berkeley: Bookworks, 1974.

Written by two practicing therapists in the Bay Area; discusses their work. Outlines feminism as healing process. Includes section on bodywork. See also Appendix B-b, Directory: Women. *Alyssum, A Center for Feminist Consciousness*.

Sarachild, Kathie. "Consciousness raising and intuition." In *The radical therapist*, ed. by J. Agel. New York: Ballantine, 1971.

"In our groups, let's share our feelings and pool them. Let's let ourselves go and see where our feelings lead us. Our feelings will lead us to ideas and then to actions."

State and Mind. (formerly *RT: A Journal of Radical Therapy*) Back issues.

Nearly all issues of Volumes four and five contain articles on feminist counselling and therapy, The Elizabeth Stone House, feminist therapy conferences, and other aspects of women and therapy. Especially recommended are: *Volume 4*, Numbers 2, 3, 5 (special women's issue), 6 and 7 (all available for $ .75 each, 2-10 at $ .60 each, 10 or more at $ .50 each); and *Volume 5*, Numbers 2 and 3 (both available for $ .75 each). Also *RT* Reprint No. 9, *Feminist Counselling* ($.50 each; $.35 for 10 or more). Order from: State and Mind (RT), P.O. Box 89, W. Somerville, Ma. 02144, U.S.A.

Williams, Elizabeth Friar. *Notes of a feminist therapist*. New York: Dell, 1977.

Some personal experiences and observations on aspects of women in therapy by a practicing New York feminst therapist. Points out the necessity for therapists to not let feminist analysis blind them to the fact that clients still often have individual problems not directly related to sexism.

Women and Therapy Collective. *Off the couch: a women's guide to therapy*. Booklet. Goddard-Cambridge Graduate Program in Social Change, 1974-5.

A practical guide with input from over 250 women at the Boston Feminist and Therapy Conference (April 1975). Covers feminist therapy theory; types of therapy and therapists; finding and interviewing therapists; the client-therapist relationship; hospitalization and alternatives; bibliography. Available for $2.00 plus $ .25 postage from RT, Inc., P.O. Box 89, W. Somerville, Mass. 02144 U.S.A.

Wyckoff, Hogie. "Radical psychiatry and transactional analysis in women's groups." Transactional Analysis Bulletin 9(36) October 1970.

A description of Hogie Wyckoff's work in women's groups. Wyckoff is associated with the Bay Area Radical Therapy and *IRT* Collectives. Her work brings together ideas from feminism, radical psychiatry and transactional analysis. See also X-d, Some Alternatives to Institutional Psychiatry: Berkeley Radical Psychiatry, for more of her writings.

Wyckoff, Hogie. "Radical psychiatry in women's groups." in *The radical therapist*, ed. by J. Agel. New York: Ballantine. 1971.

Outlines radical psychiatry principles as they apply to women working in groups.

Wyckoff, Hogie. "Amazon power workshop." *Issues in Radical Therapy* 1(4) (1973): 14-5.

Wyckoff, Hogie. "Problem-solving groups for women." *Issues in Radical Therapy* 1(1) (1973): 6-12.

Wyckoff, Hogie. *Solving women's problems.* New York: Grove Press, 1977.

"This handbook for a new self-help programme for women's personal and social problems is a blueprint for cooperative struggle which women, working together in groups, have discovered in their quest for greater power over their lives. . . its special value lies in its use as a handbook for women who wish to organize their own problem-solving group. . . ." (book cover review).

Zweig, Marilyn. "Is women's liberation a therapy group?" In *The radical therapist*, ed. by J. Agel. New York: Ballantine, 1971.

" . . . here is where the main difference between a Women's Liberation Group and a therapy group begins: our primary goal is not to attempt to help individual women find individual solutions for the problems each has in her life as a woman. We have the fundamental conviction that only a change in the life conditions of *all* women can help bring about a solution for the troubles of individual women."

e) Feminist Spirituality

Since the mid-60's the anti-psychiatry movement has had an open interest in feminist spirituality. The relationship has been complex and largely unformed, a reflection of the youthfulness and variety within this women's trend itself.

In seeking out and renewing the ancient spiritual traditions of our foremothers, women are rejecting the authoritarian, dogmatic power structure of patriarchal religions and institutions. Writers Ehrenreich and English (*Witches, Midwives and Nurses: A History of Women Healers*) point out that the present women's health movement has roots in medieval witches' covens. They describe groups of "wise women" whose access to various natural and spiritual powers laid the basis for a healing science founded on empirical study, the forerunner of modern medicine. Through a 400-year campaign of terror launched by the patriarchal ruling class, these women and their knowledge were destroyed, and a monopoly on healing came to be concentrated in the hands of the medical profession.

Some writers have linked the persecution of witches with that of mental patients. Elizabeth P. Ware Packard and Thomas Szasz, for example, draw parallels between witch-hunts of the Inquisition and the persecution of mental patients today.

Feminist spirituality groups present women with an alternative to psychiatry, a place where they receive support and validation rather than being drugged into insensitivity. They can also be used to experiment with creating cultural forms and rituals that allow emotional expression to combat the normalization and alienation of our present cultural forms. The group process is collective and offers individuals a chance to grow in an anarchic, non-authoritarian environment. It must be remembered, however, that spirituality is not itself a viable political strategy; nor is it a substitute for political action.

Anne Kent Rush's *Moon, Moon* examines the relationship between "lunacy" and matriarchal traditions; the magazine *Womanspirit* provides a forum for communicating the results of spiritual explorations among feminists today.

Daly. Mary. *Beyond God the father: toward a philosophy of women's liberation*. Boston: Beacon Press, 1973.

Daly is a major feminist theoretician on the role of patriarchal religion. This book gives a feminist analysis of "post-Christian" spirituality.

Daly, Mary. *Gyn/Ecology: the metaethics of radical feminism.* Boston: Beacon Press, 1978.

Daly, Mary. "The qualitative leap beyond patriarchal religion." *Quest: A Feminist Quarterly* (Women and Spirituality Issue) 1(4), Spring 1975.

Contains a 23 point summary of Daly's ideas, followed by a discussion of issues central to establishing a non-sexist religion.

Davis, Elizabeth G. *The first sex*. Middlesex: Penguin, 1972.

Discusses matriarchal societies and the history of the persecution of women.

Ehrenreich, Barbara and English Deirdre. *Complaints and disorders: the sexual politics of sickness*. See VII-a, Women: General Works.

Ehrenreich, Barbara and English, Deirdre. *Witches, midwives and nurses: a history of women healers.* See VII-d, Women: Feminist Therapy.

Faraday, Anne. *Dream power*. New York: Berkley, 1973.

A feminist approach to dreams that puts Freud in perspective. Argues that "you are your own dream interpreter".

Faraday, Anne. *The dream game*. New York: Harper & Row, 1974.

Feminist Wicca. *The feminist book of lights and shadows*. Available for $4.00 from: Feminist Wicca, 442 Lincoln Blvd., Venice, Ca. 90291 U.S.A.

Grimstad, Kirsten and Rennie, Susan. *The new women's survival sourcebook*. New York: Alfred A. Knopf, 1975. (Religion and Spirituality Section).

Provides excellent introduction to feminist spirituality and Wicce; critical bibliography of available literature. Includes essay, "The Old(est) Religion" which explains how, despite society's negative image and myths about witchcraft, "these days many feminists are becoming witches, and many witches are becoming feminists."

The New Broom: A Journal of Witchcraft. P.O. Box 1646, Dallas, Tx. 75221, U.S.A.

Authentic Wiccean journal with conscious feminist perspective.

Renny, Kathren. *An illustrated, annotated, feminist bibliography of Wicce, the Old Religion*. Available for $4.00 from: Pandora's Box, 250 Bowery, New York, New York 10012 U.S.A.

Comprehensive guide to witchcraft: basic literature, history, rituals, healing, and much more.

Rush, Anne Kent. *Moon, moon*. New York: Random House/San Francisco: Moon Books, 1976.

About feminist spirituality and moon lore. Contains section on lunacy—how matriarchal traditions related to moon festivities came, under patriarchal oppression, to be called "crazy", and how women were devalued by the process of calling lunar things crazy and vice versa. Also discusses the politics of spirituality. Includes sections on Moon Rituals. Discusses persection of witches and suppression of witchcraft. Surveys old mythologies. Shows how Moon Rituals, once sacred, with the advent of sun worshipping patriarchs came to be forbidden and branded madness.

Special Section on Spirituality. *State and Mind* 5(4) Nov.-Dec., 1976.

Contains 6 articles. Includes "Feminist Spirituality" by Karen Lindsey, which discusses the growing spirituality movement within feminist culture and some ongoing arguments between "spiritualists" and "politicos". Also includes Ahshe Green's letter outlining the need for a women's spiritual movement as distinct from the male spiritual movement.

Szasz, Thomas S. *The manufacture of madness: a comparative study of the Inquisition and the mental health movement*. New York: Dell, 1971. Chapter 6: The Witch as Healer.

Valiente, Doreen. *A B C of Witchcraft*. New York: St. Martin's Press, 1973.

Resource book on the practice of the Old Religion by long experienced practioner, illustrated.

Womanspirit. See XI-e, General and Misc.: Periodicals.

Women and Spirituality Issue. *Quest: A Feminist Quarterly* 1(4), Spring, 1975. Available for $2.00 from: Quest, A Feminist Quarterly, P.O. Box 8843, Washington D.C. 20003 U.S.A.

VIII. Psychiatry and
STILL WORKING...
other
oppressed
groups

VIII PSYCHIATRY AND OTHER OPPRESSED GROUPS

Most of the writings in this section deal with specific groups of oppressed people, examining how they are oppressed by society in general and by psychiatry/psychology in particular.

Going beyond the difference in their individual situations, many oppressed groups are now linking their struggles together, both theoretically and in practice. They have come to see how the ruling class keeps us fragmented into little groups, hating, fearing, and fighting *each other* instead of fighting back collectively.

The psychiatric system is a powerful tool in this divide and conquor strategy. Its operations perpetuate the myths and conditions that foster sexism, racism, classism, ageism, and mentalism in a society based on competitiveness, exploitation, and greed rather than sharing and co-operation. Psychiatry has developed a pseudo-science to assert the so-called inferiority of large groups of people. To help keep these people in line, it is prepared to use its most violent weapons of social control: drugging, electroshock, psychosurgery, etc. First, however, it teaches everyone to internalize their oppression and to perceive it as a personal problem, "complex", or "disease", Its technology of normalization forces us to identify with our oppressors and internalize their values. Psychiatry, with its lies couched in an elusive, pseudo-scientific jargon, keeps us forever mystified about ourselves and about each other. And thus a small ruling minority is helped to maintain its stranglehold over the lives of a vast majority of people.

Writings of the black militants have provided valuable inspiration to other oppressed groups. In particular, Frantz Fanon's work on colonialism and revolution in Algeria represents a beginning framework for the psychology of oppressed peoples, and shows how *true* mental health can only be achieved through revolution.

a) Third World

No comprehensive and definitive anti-psychiatry work yet exists in the area of psychiatric oppression of Third World people. Works such as Thomas and Sillen's *Racism and Psychiatry* have made a start. While many of the writings listed here attack institutionalized racism within the mental health system, they stop short because they are sexist in outlook, still cling to a number of white middle-class values, and don't really attack the psychiatric system as a whole. This section also includes writings of feminists who analyze the sexism in male Third World writings.

The works of Frantz Fanon are especially important documents which explore the psychology of oppressed peoples living under colonial rule.

Some important current issues facing Third World people include the following psychiatric menaces: the spreading of racist I.Q. theories by social scientists (also see V-f: Psychological Testing); the recent upsurge of psychosurgery and its implications for ghetto residents who, according to three leading psychosurgeons, should be "screened for violence" and given their psychosurgery (also see V-b: Psychosurgery); and the overly disproportionate number of Third World persons incarcerated in mental hospitals, prisons, and "adjustment centers".

The American Journal of Insanity. "Madness and blackness." In *The age of madness: the history of involuntary mental hospitalization presented in selected texts*, ed. by T.S.Szasz. Garden City, New York: Doubleday/Anchor, 1973.

Extracted from essay published in 1851. Reviews 1840 census and concludes that the "principal abodes of idiocy and lunacy" are among the free colored population, as compared to whites and slaves.

Beal, Frances. "Double jeopardy: to be black and female." In *Female liberation: history and current politics*, ed. by Roberta Salper. New York: Alfred A. Knopf, 1972.

Discusses the effects of racism, capitalism, and sexism on the black woman in America from feminist perspective. Questions many white middle-class male values that most black male writers seem to take for granted in their psychological analyses of racism.

Bickley, Richard. "Race, class and the I.Q. controversy." See V-f, Mind Control: Psychological Testing.

Burris, Barbara (in agreement with Kathy Barry, Terry Moon, Joann DeLor, Joann Parent, Cate Stadelman) "The fourth world manifesto." In *Notes from the third year: women's liberation,* ed. by Anne Koedt and Shulamith Firestone. (Available from: Notes, P.O. Box AA, Old Chelsea Station, New York, N.Y. 10011 U.S.A.)

Analyzes position of women cross-culturally and shows how all anti-capitalist, anti-imperialist, Third World, etc. movements have proved thus far to be male-defined and a dead end for women. Includes good study of Frantz Fanon, exposing his ubiquitous sexism and identification with male-supremacist culture. Gives a clear picture of how, during revolutions, women have had to play the role of pawn between two fighting male cultures.

Carmichael Stokley, "Black power." In *To free a nation: the dialectics of liberation*, ed. by D. Cooper. Middlesex: Penguin, 1968.

Discusses factors behind race oppression and liberation. Says that it is a cop-out to think in terms of the individual and that the capitalist system of white supremacy must be smashed.

Chesler, Phyllis. *Women and madness*. New York: Avon Books, 1973.Chapter 8: Third World Women.

Discusses the psychology of racism as it relates to women. Examines several works on the psychology of racism that were written by males and are disappointingly sexist. Points out the difficulty of *documenting* racist practices in the selection and treatment of the "mentally ill". Includes interviews with female psychiatric patients of African and Latin-American descent.

Dormaar, N.G. "Indian health in a white man's society." *British Columbia Medical Journal* 16(11) (1974): 1-2.

Dr. Dormaar of Williams Lake, British Columbia (Canada) visited the Vancouver Mental Patients Association in 1973 to investigate and study the effectiveness of "power-reversal" for mental patients and its possible application to Indian health care.

Fanon, Frantz. *A dying colonialism*. Trans. by Haakon Chevalier. New York: Grove Press, 1967.

Fanon was a black psychiatrist from the French colony of Martinique and participated in the Algerian revolution; his works are important pioneer studies in the psychology of oppressed peoples. Working from a revolutionary and Marxist viewpoint, he shows how the mental illness of colonial people is a result of their oppression and that mental health comes from revolution. His work does not go far enough, though and Fanon remains totally oblivious to the colonized status of the brothers' "women".

Fanon, Frantz. *The wretched of the earth*. Trans. by Constance Farrington. New York: Grove Press, 1965.

Shows relationship between mental health and revolution.

Fanon, Frantz. *Black skin, white masks*. Trans. by Charles L. Markmann. New York: Grove Press, 1967.

Shows the psychological destruction of oppressed colonial peoples.

Fanon, Frantz. *Toward the African revolution*. New York: Grove Press, 1968.

Fanon, Frantz. "The so-called dependency complex in colonized people." In *Radical psychology*, ed. by P. Brown. New York: Harper & Row, 1973.

Excerpt from *Black Skins, White Masks*.

Fanon, Frantz. "Concerning violence." In *Radical psychology*, ed. by P. Brown. New York: Harper & Row, 1973.

Excerpt from *The Wretched of the Earth*.

Hernton, Calvin C. *Sex and racism in America.* New York: Grove Press, 1966.

A black sociologist looks at the problems of sex and racism in America and suggests some male middle-class theories to explain the black woman, whom he regards as domineering and castrating.

Kovel, Joel. *White racism: a psychohistory.* New York: Random House/ Vintage, 1971.

Presents a pessimistic theory of contemporary America.

Piercy, Marge. *Woman on the edge of time*. See I-b, The Mental Patient Experience: General Fiction.

Racism and Aging Issue. *Psychiatric Opinion* 10(6) December 1973.

Special issue devoted to the elderly black.

Third World Issue. Madness Network News 3(5) March 1976.

This special issue of *MNN* was edited by a Third World staff from a Third World perspective. Language and content were geared toward a Third World understanding of psychiatric oppression. Emphasis is on Blacks in America but also includes an article by an Asian Sister. Contains a 2-page listing of Third World community services.

Thomas, Alexander and Sillen, Samuel. *Racism and psychiatry*. New York: Brunner-Mazel, 1972.

Pioneer exploration of institutionalizated racism in the mental health system.

Torrey, E.F. "Mental health services for American Indians and Eskimos." *Community Health Journal* 6(6) (1970): 455-63.

Ware, Celestine. "Black feminism." In *Notes from the third year: women's liberation*, ed. by Anne Koedt and Shulamith Firestone. (Available from: Notes, P.O. Box AA, Old Chelsea Station, New York, N.Y. 10011 U.S.A.) Adapted from Ware's *Woman Power: The Movement for Women's Liberation*. New York: Tower Books, 1970.

Explodes the myth of the "black bitch" and other stereotypes that writers such as Hernton perpetuate.

b) The Poor

There have been a number of good sociological studies on social class and mental illness. Among them, two of the best known classics are Hollingshead and Redlich's *Social Class and Mental Illness* and the Cornell Midtown Study. While statistics vary somewhat from study to study, what the research in this field clearly reveals is that the overwhelming majority of psychiatric patients come from the lowest socioeconomic stratum and that poverty-induced stress causes emotional disturbance.

These studies also discredit the so-called "drift hypothesis" which alleges that mentally ill persons "drift" downward socially because of their "nature". At the same time, they demonstrate how many of the "symptoms" of "schizophrenia" are actually natural responses to being trapped in the intolerable conditions of slum life. Harrington's classic, *The Other America*, gives a detailed portrait of the poor living in the United States and shows how American society perpetuates this culture of misery.

Psychiatric treatment itself is also different for the poor than for the rich. Psychiatric patients with money are less often incarcerated and usually receive private attention from a psychotherapist or analyst. They are less apt to be labelled "psychotic" or "schizophrenic". The poor, on the other hand, are more frequently incarcerated, often involuntarily, and are more apt to be given physical forms of treatment such as drugging and electroshock.

Braginsky, D.D. and Braginsky, B.M. "Surplus people: their lost faith in self and system." *Psychology Today* 9(3), August, 1975.

Chesler, Phyllis. *Women and madness*. New York: Avon, 1973. Appendix: The Female Career as a Psychiatric Patient: The Sex, Class, Race, and Marital Status of America's Psychiatrically Involved Population, 1950-1969.

Presents data tables and explains problems involved in interpreting them. Points out flaws in studies such as Hollingshead and Redlich.

Coles, Robert. *Children of crisis.* Boston: Little & Brown, 1964.

A community psychiatrist documents the effects of racism and poverty on people's mental "health". Clearly describes the system of social injustices. Coles questions the validity of the medical model.

Coles, R. and Huge, H. "Strom Thurmond Country: the way it is in South Carolina." *New Republic* (November 30, 1968): 17-21.

An article exposing conditions of poverty and demanding rectification. It received wide publicity and led to implementation of food stamps and other changes.

Colletti, Anthony. " 'Schizophrenia' and poverty." *State and Mind* 6(4) and 7(1) Summer/Fall 1978.

A good overview of literature in the area, this article ties together evidence of "how social policy and mental health theory and practice perpetuate poverty-induced stress." Includes discussion of "Poverty Profiteers". Written by American east coast mental patients activist.

Dohrenwend, Bruce and Dohrenwend, Barbara. *Social status and psychological disorders*. New York: John Wiley, 1969.

Duhl, L.J. "The shame of the cities." *American Journal of Psychiatry* 124(9) (1968): 1184-9.

American community psychiatrist exposes how cities are causing psychiatric problems. Although using medical metaphors in places, Duhl came to question the validity of the medical model.

Elman, Richard M. *The poorhouse state: the American way of life on public assistance*. New York: Dell, 1976.

Exposes welfare system. Uses study of the "welfare ghetto" of New York's Lower East Side as point of departure. Shows how welfare programs create and perpetuate the poverty they set out to alleviate.

Harrington, Michael. *The other America: poverty in the United States.* Baltimore: Penguin, 1971.

A classic work on "the new poverty" in post-depression America. Easily readable, this book explores the day-to-day lives of the poor and shows how the social structure enforces this self-perpetuating culture. Chapter 7 is a discussion of emotional disturbance and poverty, reviewing some of the classic studies and literature.

Hollingshead, A.B. and Redlich, F.C. *Social class and mental illness: a community study*. New York: Wiley, 1958.

A classic in its field. Reports on the first part of a research study on interrelations between social stratification and mental illness in a New England community (the second part is found in J.K. Myers and B.H. Roberts, *Family and Class Dynamics in Mental Illness*). Their findings indicate that social class is related significantly to: 1) the prevalence of treated psychiatric disorders; 2) the types of treated psychiatric disorders; and 3) the type of therapy administered. This study shows that statistically, the majority of institutionalized patients belong in the lowest socioeconomic class.

Hollingshead,A.B., Myers, J.K. and Yahreas, H. "Social class and mental illness: a follow-up study." In *Behavioural sciences and mental health*, ed. by E.A. Rubenstein and G.V. Coelho. Washington: U.S. Department of Health, Education and Welfare, 1970.

Kohn, Melvin K. "Social class and schizophrenia." *Schizophrenia Bulletin,* National Institute of Mental Health, Winter 1973.

A review of past studies of social class and mental illness. Concludes that "in all probability, more schizophrenia is actually produced at the lowest socio-economic levels."

Marx, Karl. "Alienated labor." In *Radical psychology*, ed. by P. Brown. New York: Harper & Row, 1973.

Classic Marxist document (excerpted from *Economic and Philosophic Manuscripts of 1844*) analyzes how labour in a capitalist system causes alienation of the workers. This viewpoint is, of course, totally at odds with the rationale of "work therapy" programs being massively enforced in psychiatric institutions today.

Myers, J.K. and Bean, L.L. *A decade later: a follow-up of social class and mental illness*. New York: Wiley, 1968.

Myers, J.K. and Roberts, B.H. *Family class dynamics in mental illness*. New York: Wiley, 1959.

The second part of *Social Class and Mental Illness* (Hollingshead and Redlich). Findings reported here support the hypothesis that social and psychodynamic factors in the development of psychiatric disorders are correlative to an individual's position in the class structure; and support, in part, the hypothesis that mobility in the class structure is associated with the development of psychiatric disorders.

Rogler, Lloyd H. and Hollingshead, August B. *Trapped: families and schizophrenia*. New York: Wiley, 1965.

"This book examines the intimate, detailed life histories of a series of families who live in the slums and public housing projects of San Juan, Puerto Rico." It explores the many complex factors surrounding the onset and course of mental illness in this population.

Roman, Paul M. and Trice, Harrison M. *Schizophrenia and the poor*. Ithaca: New York State School of Industrial and Labor Relations, Cornell University, 1967.

A review of the literature on mental disorder and social status. Reports how the literature under review shows that persons defined as having mental disorders are generally found in the lowest social stratum. The authors conclude that: "There appears to be a direct causal relationship between the fact of economic deprivation and the stress and disorganization present at this level" and that the frustrations experienced by persons in this situation figure a major part in the development of "schizophrenia" and similar mental problems.

Smith, Dorothy E. "The statistics on mental illness: what they will not tell us about women and why." In *Women look at psychiatry*, ed. by D. Smith and S. David. Vancouver: Press Gang Publishers, 1975.

A good primer on how to read mental health statistics and how to read out the lies often built into them, especially as they pertain to Canadian statistics and women.

Scrole, Leo et al. *Mental health in the metropolis: Midtown Manhattan study.* New York: McGraw-Hill, 1962.

A report of the famous Cornell Midtown study, one of the most comprehensive studies of social class and mental illness. It develops a series of "stress factors" and shows how poverty-induced stress contributes to mental breakdown.

c) Children

Politically, children are powerless. There are few, if any, non-oppressive therapy models for kids with problems in living—either in theory or practice. The current trends are drugging and behaviour modification programs. More and more, medical ideology is being called upon to define children's nonconformity behaviour, and medical technology used to control it. Massive "screening" and labelling programs are also being expanded today for the purpose of weeding out potential troublemakers and to train a docile next generation: children as young as five are enrolled in U.S. federal government sponsored "pre-delinquency" programs.

Braginsky, B.M. & Braginsky, D.D. "The mentally retarded: society's Hansels and Gretels." *Psychology Today* 7(10) (March 1974): 18-30.

Exposes society's myths about mental retardation. Shows how the label of "mentally retarded" gets conveniently applied to individuals by a family who has decided to remove them. Shows how so-called "retarded" persons can vary their I.Q. and that retardation is a myth used to justify institutionalization of an unwanted child.

Braginsky, D.D. & Braginsky, B.M. *Hansels and Gretels: studies of children in institutions.* New York: Holt, Rinehart & Winston, 1971.

Braginsky, D.D. & Braginsky, B.M. "The intelligent behavior of mental retardates: a study of their manipulation of intelligence and test scores." *Journal of Personality* 40(40) (December 1972): 558-63.

Breggin, Peter. "Underlying a method. Is psychosurgery an acceptable treatment for hyperactivity in children?" *Mental Hygiene* 58 (Winter 1974): 19-21.

Chabasinski, Ted. "Growing up in a mental hospital." In *Madness unmasked,* ed. by Mental Patients Association. Vancouver: Mental Patients Publishing Project, 1974.

Autobiographical account of Network Against Psychiatric Assault activist's childhood at Rockland State Hospital. Chabasinski was incarcerated when he was six years old and became one of the first children to be "treated" with electric shock: his confinement lasted ten years.

Children's Issue. *Madness Network News* 3(2) 1976. (Back issues available for 50¢ each from: Madness Network News, Box 684, San Francisco, Ca. 94101, U.S.A.)

Children's Rights Workshop, 1970 Berkeley Conference. "The rights of children: recommendations." In *The radical therapist*, ed. by J. Agel. New York: Ballantine, 1971.

Caligari, Dr. "Child druggers." *Madness Network News* 3(6) (1976): 16-17.

Reports the latest news about child control scene with predictions for the coming decade. Includes excerpts from various journals, books, reports, etc.

Crisis in child mental health: a critical assessment. Available from: Group for the Advancement of Psychiatry, 419 Park Ave. South, New York, N.Y. 10016, U.S.A.

This 1972 study criticizes the government's Report of the Joint Commission on Mental Health of Children and makes recommendations on what is needed to improve child mental health services.

Dabrowski, Kazimerez. *Positive disintegration.* Ed. with Introduction by Jason Aronson. Boston: Little, Brown & Company, 1964. Chapter 8: Positive Disintegration and Child Development.

Dabrowski relates so-called clinical symptoms of childhood mental illness to his theory of positive disintegration. Besides his work in personality theory, Dabrowski's career was also much involved with the study of child psychiatry.

Druikers, Rudolf & Grey, Loren. *Logical consequences: a new approach to discipline.* New York: Meredith Press, 1968.

Essentially an educational model for behavior change in children. It presents a system built around the principle of responsible decision-making — offering children choices of behavior and giving them responsibility for the consequences of the choice they make — instead of engaging in power struggles and demanding forced obedience. This model provides learning experiences in how to use power, and relates consequences to decision-making and personal action rather than to the whims of adults.

FPS: A Magazine of Young People's Liberation. See XI-e, Periodicals.

Nowicki, Victor. "Legal speed for kids." *In A Nutshell: Mental Patients Association Newsletter* 4(2) (May 1976): 1-3.

Exposes myths of "hyperactivity" and the ignorance of the medical profession. Attacks child drugging; exposes the economics of drug companies; reveals the dangers of Ritalin.

Schrag, Peter & Divorky, Diane. *The myth of the hyper-active child: and other means of child control.* New York: Dell, 1976.

Already a classic, this book is essential reading for anyone seeking to get informed about current scene of how psychiatric ideology and technology are being used to invade children's lives. Contains extensive bibliography.

Special Children's Issue. *RT: A Journal of Radical Therapy* 5(1) 1976.

van Stolk, Mary. *The battered child in Canada.* Toronto: McClelland & Stewart, 1972.

Primer of child abuse in Canada. Discusses facts, statistics, medical aspects, and legal issues. Gives social class profiles and examines other social issues. Includes section on rights and limits of parenthood.

Youth Liberation. *Youth liberation: news, politics, and survival information.* Albion, Ca.: Times Change Press, 1972.

Contains some of the best articles from early issues of *FPS.* Includes original Youth Liberation platform and personal statements from young people on the need to struggle for liberation. Available for $1.75 from: Youth Liberation, 2007 Washtenaw Avenue, Ann Arbor, Mi. 48104, U.S.A.

Youth Liberation Pamphlets. Available for $.75 plus 50¢ postage each (25¢ postage for additional copies; postage free on orders over $5.00) from: Youth Liberation, 2007 Washtenaw Avenue, Ann Arbor, Mi. 48104, U.S.A.

These pamphlets contain articles, bibliography and resource material listings.

d) Gays

In the era of psychiatric power, according to Thomas Szasz (*The Manufacture of Madness*), the homosexual has been given the role of "model psychiatric scapegoat" who could be accused of both crime and disease. But gays have grown tired of psychiatry's century-long monologue defining their lifestyle as a "disease" and, in 1970, militants began a series of public confrontations with the psychiatric profession.

Efforts of the gay liberation movement have yielded results: the "crime" of homosexuality was removed from lawbooks in some areas of the world and, on Dec. 14, 1973, the American Psychiatric Association eliminated homosexuality from its official *Diagnostic and Statistical Manual of Mental Disorders*.

A genuine beginning to the end of gay oppression? Not exactly. A poll taken several months after the APA policy change revealed that 40% of American shrinks did not really agree with the move, claiming there was no "scientific" evidence to support it (see Charles Socarides, "Beyond sexual freedom"). And in practice, of course, psychiatrists and other mental health professionals continue to "treat" gays for their homosexuality with both traditional high-priced analysis, and contemporary behaviour mod programs involving various punishment techniques. The article by Louis Landerson provides frightening documentation of some "aversive" techniques now in use.

In the late 70's gay people have also become the primary scapegoat for a new right-wing movement which, in America, has contributed the category of "sin" to the list that already includes crime and disease. The psychiatric establishment, by persisting in regarding and treating homosexuals as deviants, has provided much of the ideological impetus for this offensive.

Throughout the history of the gay movement, there has been a predominance of male gay activists. This is partly due to male chauvinsim within the movement itself, and partly due to many lesbian activists finding they could better fight their oppression using the context and support of the women's movement. Hence, most of the writings in this section pertain to gay men and/or gay issues in general. See also VII-b, Lesbians.

Altman, Dennis. *Homosexual: oppression and liberation.* New York: Outerbridge & Dienstfrey, 1971.

The Body Politic. See XI-e, Periodicals.

Boggan, E. et al. *The rights of gay people.* See III-d, Patients Rights.

Diamon, N.A. "Toward a gay psychology." *Issues in Radical Therapy* 1(4) October, 1973.

A gay bibliography: basic materials on homosexuality. Prepared by Task Force on Gay Liberation, Social Responsibilities Round Table, American Library Association. Free copies available on request with stamped reply envelope from: Barbara Gittings, Coordinator, P.O. Box 2383, Philadelphia, Pa. 19103, U.S.A.

Lists books, periodicals, pamphlets, and articles. Includes material on both gay women and men. Revised periodically.

Gay People and Mental Health. See XI-e, Periodicals.

Hobson, Christopher Z. "Surviving psychotherapy." In *Rough times,* ed. by J. Agel. New York: Ballantine, 1973.

Autobiographical account by a gay man of his experiences of oppressive "therapy" with psychiatrist.

Homosexual Counselling Journal. See XI-e, Periodicals.

Kameny, Franklin E. "Gay liberation and psychiatry." In *The homosexual dialectic,* ed. by J. McCaffrey. Englewood Cliffs, N.J.: Prentice-Hall, 1972.

Well known leader in gay movement discusses relationship between gay liberation and psychiatry from gay perspective.

Landerson, Louis/Liberation News Service. "Psychiatry and homosexuality: new 'cures'." In *Rough times,* ed. by J. Agel. New York: Ballantine, 1973.

Describes techniques currently being developed for psychiatric "treatment" of male homosexuals. Psychosurgery involving implanted electrodes in the brain is one such "breakthrough"; aversive conditioning therapy is another area opening up. This latter form of behavior mod includes a range of standard punishment media from drugs (succinylcholine and apomorphine) to electricity (wiring the genitals with electrodes to administer a shock whenever response to photo of naked male occurs – the "Errorless Extinction of Penile Responses").

McCaffrey, Joseph A., ed. *The homosexual dialectic.* See XI-b, Anthologies.

McCubbin, Bob. *The gay question: a Marxist analysis.* Available for $1 from: World View Publishers, 46 W. 21st St., New York, N.Y. 10010, U.S.A.

". . .'traces and links the roots of gay oppression to the overthrow of the matriarchy and the rise of class society.' The main theme of the 85-page booklet is that persecution of homosexuals did not exist in a pre-class society characterized by sharing and equality in human relationships; the author then argues that socialist revolution is necessary for a return to those non-oppressive conditions." (the Librarian, *State and Mind* 5(5) 1977.)

Pearlman, David. "The psychiatrists and the protestors." In *Toward social change: a handbook for those who will,* ed. by R. Buckhout et al. New York: Harper & Row, 1971. (Reprinted from the *San Francisco Chronicle,* May 24, 1970.)

Describes confrontation at 1970 annual meeting of the American Psychiatric Association by members of Women's Liberation and the Gay Liberation Front, who protested the APA's sexual chauvinism and insensitive treatment of homosexuals and women.

Psychiatry and the homosexual: a brief analysis of oppression. Gay Liberation Pamphlet No. 1, 1973. Available from: Pomegranate Press, 165 Gloucester Avenue, London N.W. 1, England.

Written by a collective of men, this pamphlet examines the treatment of homosexuality by mainstream psychiatry and explodes some popular myths about gays.

Socarides, Charles W. "Beyond sexual freedom: clinical fallout." *American Journal of Psychotherapy* 30(3) 1976.

Sexist and reactionary shrink discusses the American Psychiatric Association's removal of homosexuality from its *Diagnostic and Statistical Manual of Mental Disorders.* Includes results and summary of a poll taken of American shrinks and how a large number of them still believe that homosexuality is a disease.

Szasz, Thomas S. "Legal and moral aspects of homosexuality." In *Sexual inversion: the multiple roots of homosexuality*, ed. by J. Marmor. New York: Basic Books, 1965.

Szasz, Thomas S. *The manufacture of madness: a comparative study of the Inquisition and the mental health movement.* New York: Dell, 1970. Chapter 10: The Product Conversion – From Heresy to Illness and Chapter 13: The Model Psychiatric Scapegoat – The Homosexual.

Gives Szaszian analysis of homosexual's position in modern society. Shows how the homosexual is regarded today in the same way as was the heretic by the Church. Describes double jeopardy of homosexuals, who can be accused of both crime and "disease".

Teal, Don. *The gay militants.* New York: Stein & Day, 1971.

A history of early years of American gay liberation movement. Mostly about men's gay liberation except for one chapter which was contributed by lesbians. Includes accounts of gay confrontation with American Psychiatric Association (May 14, 1970) in San Francisco and at other professional conferences held to read papers on "homosexuality" and give lectures on aversion therapy.

Tobin, Kay & Wicker, Randy. *The gay crusaders.* New York: Paperback Library, 1972.

Stories about gay liberation activists and their groups. Includes interviews. "Our resistance signals the first time in the history of psychiatry that a class of people defined as having a psychiatric problem has stood up to its self-appointed benefactors and rejected the 'help' they wanted so avidly to give. . . . For almost a century psychiatry has poisoned the whole climate of thinking about homosexuality!" (Barbara Gittings on Gay Liberation's confrontations with the American Psychiatric Association's 1970 and 1971 annual conventions)

Wittman, Carl. "Gay liberation manifesto." In *The radical therapist,* ed. by J. Agel. New York: Ballantine, 1971.

Defines and discusses (in point form) some of the central gay issues: sexual orientation, women, roles, oppression, and coalition.

Youth Liberation. *Growing up gay.* Pamphlet. Available for 75¢ postage from Youth Liberation (see Appendix B-c).

Contains articles relevant to teenage gays and lesbians coming out in high school. Includes good bibliography.

e) Political Dissidents

Methods of psychiatric abuse are being employed for purposes of political repression in many areas of the world today. Communist states, fascist dictatorships and "free" countries alike have been finding psychiatry a convenient tool for silencing voices of opposition to their regimes.

Among the current literature on psychiatric political repression, reports from the Soviet Union seem to be both the most numerous and best publicized. These reports, usually personal testimonies unofficially written and secretly smuggled out of the USSR, began reaching the West in the early 1960's. They describe how sane citizens had been railroaded into mental institutions because they openly criticized the Russian bureaucracy. Once inside these psychiatric prisons, the dissenters were coerced with beatings, heavy drugging, physical restraints, etc. The cases of Leonid Pluysch, Vladimir Bukovsky, and Zhores Medvedev are three of the better known ones in the West.

While the West has given a great deal of publicity to Soviet abuses of psychiatry, it has tended to ignore and suppress evidence of parallels in its own countries (see Henley and *Madness Network News* "Editorial"). Recent examples of psychiatric repression in the West include the case of Anna R., a Swiss nuclear power protester, and mind control programs largely aimed at Third World people in American ghettos and prisons.

Another area now flourishing is Latin America, where the Argentinian *Junta* has reportedly enlisted psychiatry to help enforce its reign of terror.

Abuse of psychiatry for political repression in the Soviet Union. Vol. 1 & 2. Washington, D.C.: U.S. Government Printing Office, 1972, 1975.

Chalidze, Valery. *To defend these rights.* New York: Random House, 1975.

Documents psychiatric repression in the USSR.

Committee for the Defense of Soviet Political Prisoners. *The abuse of psychiatry in the USSR: Soviet dissenters in psychiatric prisons.* Pamphlet. New York: CDSPP Press, 1976. Available for 75¢ from: P.O. Box 142, Cooper Station, New York, N.Y. 10003, U.S.A.

Includes profiles and testimonies by prisoners, documenting their experiences; Bukovsky and Gluzman's document, "A Manual of Psychiatry for Dissidents"; partial list of current prisoners; selected bibliography and list of defense committees.

Committee for the Defense of Soviet Political Prisoners. *Inside Soviet prisons.* Pamphlet. New York: CDSPP Press, 1976.

Committee for the Defense of Soviet Political Prisoners. *Political prisoners in the USSR: who they are, what they stand for, how you can help them.* Pamphlet. (Adrian Karatnychy, ed.) New York: CDSPP Press, 1975.

Committee for the Defense of Soviet Political Prisoners. *Women political prisoners in the USSR.* Pamphlet. New York: CDSPP Press, 1975.

Gorbanyevskaya, Natalia. *Red square at noon.* London: Andre Deutsch, 1972.

Documents psychiatric repression in the USSR.

Henley, Nancy. "Back in the USSR: the politics of psychiatry." In *Rough times,* ed. by J. Agel. New York: Ballantine, 1973.

Summarizes and discusses attempts made during the early 1970's in the "free" world to protest abuses of Russian psychiatry. Comments on how the U.S. eagerly publicizes the atrocities of Soviet psychiatric suppression of dissidents while blatantly neglecting to mention parallels in its own country.

"Human experimentation, psychiatry, and the press." Editorial. *Madness Network News.* See V-g, Mind Control: General & Misc.

Kaiser, Steve & Koren, Sheila. "New trends in Argentinian psychiatry," News Shorts, *State and Mind* 6(1) (Fall 1977): 3.

A very brief report outlining how the *Junta* of Argentina is using psychiatry in its arsenal of torture methods to strengthen its reign over the country.

Marchenko, Anatoly. *My testimony.* New York: E.P. Dutton & Co., 1969.

Documents psychiatric repression in the Soviet Union.

Medvedev, Zhores & Medvedev, Roy. *A question of madness.* Trans. by Ellen de Kadt. New York: Knopf, 1971.

The chronicle of Zhores Medvedev, Soviet biochemist and outspoken critic of Soviet bureaucracy, who was railroaded into mental hospital. His brother rallied Soviet intellectual community in protest to tell the story of what goes on in Russian psychiatry. Form of dual autobiographical account leading to Medvedev's eventual conditional release. This case has received much publicity in the west and was frequently cited in the protest literature.

Mills, Bruce. "Report on Soviet psychiatry." *In A Nutshell: Mental Patients Association Newsletter* 6(1) March, 1978.

Gives a brief background to current uses of Soviet psychiatry as "the Kremlin's subtle tool."

Prisoners of conscience in the USSR: their treatment and conditions. London: Amnesty International Publications, 1975.

Psychiatric abuse of political prisoners in the Soviet Union — testimony by Leonid Pluysch. Washington, D.C.: U.S. Government Printing Office, 1976.

Reddaway, Peter, ed. *Uncensored Russia.* New York: American Heritage, 1972.

Saunders, George, ed. *Samizdat, voices of Soviet opposition.* New York: Monad Press, 1974.

Tarsis, Valery. *Ward 7.* See I-a, Autobiographical Accounts.

Temkin, Tanya. "Electroshock: punishment for protest. . ." *Madness Network News* 4(6) Spring, 1978.

A report on the case of "Anna R.", a young Swiss woman who was forcibly incarcerated in a mental hospital and given electroshock after taking part in a protest against nuclear power.

f) Oppressed Groups: General & Misc.

The aged and community health: a guide to program development. Report, 1971. Available from: Committee on Aging, Group for the Advancement of Psychiatry, 419 Park Ave. South, New York, N.Y. 10016, U.S.A.

Aldebaron, Mayer. *Fat liberation.* Available for $.50 (bulk rates available) from: Issues in Radical Therapy Press, P.O. Box 23544, Oakland, Ca. 94623, U.S.A.

An article exploding the myths about fatness and exposing fat oppression.

The Fat Underground. *Fat Liberation Manifesto.* Available from: The Fat Underground, 1102-1104 W. Washington Boulevard, Venice, Ca. 90291, U.S.A.
Exposes how the medical, psychiatric, industrial, and advertising professions exploit and oppress fat people – especially women.

Friedman, Paul R. *The rights of mentally retarded persons.* See III-d, Patients Rights.

Goffman, Erving. *Stigma: notes on the management of spoiled identity.* See II-b: Other Social/Phenomenological Studies.

Hamalian, Leo & Karl, Frederick R., eds. *The fourth world: the poor, the sick, the elderly and underaged in America.* See XI-b: Anthologies.

Statman, Jim. "Community Mental Health as a pacification program." In *The radical therapist,* ed. by J. Agel, New York: Ballantine, 1971.

Examines political and social functions of community mental health programs in urban ghettos.

Torrey, E. Fuller. *The death of psychiatry.* New York: Penguin, 1975. Chapter 7: Mental Disease As Preventable: The Road to Psychiatric Fascism.

Psychiatry, by using the medical model, was able to extend its scope to "preventive psychiatry". Torrey examines how this concept has been largely accepted and supported by both the medical profession and those sponsoring "community mental health", then goes on to show that this setup allows psychiatrists almost unlimited power to intrude into people's lives in the community (and more specifically in ghettos). Further on in the book (p. 152-3) Torrey examines how psychiatric fascism has even been extended to old people so that old age can be defined as an "illness", and old persons as "sick" and in need of being sent off to "hospitals".

IX. The Mental Patients
FREE ALL
PSYCHIATRIC
INMATES
Liberation Movement

IX THE MENTAL PATIENTS' LIBERATION MOVEMENT

a) Mental Patients' Liberation Fronts

The Mental Patients' Liberation Movement began emerging at the grassroots level early in 1971. In North America, the three earliest groups, New York Mental Patients Liberation Project (MPLP), Vancouver Mental Patients Association (M.P.A.) and Boston Mental Patients Liberation Front (MPLF) sprang up almost simultaneously yet independent of each other.

Although Mental Patients Liberation groups vary in both their activities and their political stands on some issues, they share a basic solidarity of purpose: to abolish the psychiatric system as it now stands. As the name suggests, the movement focuses on more than patients' rights, and has taken on the task of evolving its own political analysis of psychiatric oppression, an analysis that has extended to a strong condemnation of the entire social system. The movement sees parallels between itself and other liberation groups, such as the Prison movement, Women's and Gay Liberation, and the anti-imperialist movement in general.

Boston MPLF is a good example of an active established group. Run entirely by ex-psychiatric inmates (exceptions are rare) and existing on next to no money, Boston MPLF conducts such activities as: lobbying for patients' rights, visiting and counselling inmates in hospitals, publishing and distributing information, and public speaking. Another prominent American group is Network Against Psychiatric Assault (NAPA), which was formed in 1974 by people who came together through *Madness Network News*. It now has several chapters throughout California. NAPA puts a lot of focus on campaigning against electro-shock, psychosurgery, unpaid labour in institutions, and all involuntary treatment. The Vancouver Mental Patients Association, which has evolved somewhat differently from most other groups, is discussed in X-b. In Great Britain, there exists a Federation of Mental Patients Unions. They have mainly organized around improving the rights of people incarcerated in mental institutions. The London MPU keeps a list of individuals and groups active in England, Wales, and Scotland.

The few writings listed here are mainly of a general interest nature; further information about specific mental patients liberation groups can be obtained by writing to addresses listed in Appendix B: Directory.

State and Mind and *Madness Network News* are two of the best sources of movement news; they provide good coverage for group activities and advertise new groups forming. *State and Mind* is especially good for U.S. east coast news, *MNN* for the west coast and Bay area. See XI-e, Periodicals.

Brown, Phil. *Towards a Marxist psychology*. New York: Harper & Row, 1974. Pages 143-6: "The Mental Patients Liberation Movement". (For more information about this book, see XI-a, Anti-Psychiatry: General Works.)

Frankfort, Ellen. *Vaginal Politics*. See VII-a, Women: General Works.

Insane Liberation Front. In *The radical therapist*, ed. by J. Agel. New York: Ballantine, 1971.

Statement and Demands from *Insane Manifesto*.

Mental Patients Liberation. RT Reprint No. 1. Available for $ .50 each ($ .40 each for nine or more) from: RT, Inc., P.O. Box 89, W. Somerville, Ma. 02114 U.S.A.

Statements written at the inception of two of the earliest ex-mental patients' groups (New York Mental Patients' Liberation Front, Vancouver Mental Patients Association).

Mental Patients' Rights and Organizing Issue. *Rough Times* 3(2), November, 1972. Back issues available for $ .50 each from: RT, Inc., P.O. Box 89, W. Somerville, Ma. 02144 U.S.A.

Contains statements by and information on most of the mental patients' liberation groups active during late 1972. Good for a summary of what was going on (issues, problems, tactics) during early days of the movement in North America.

New York Mental Patients' Project. "Mental Patients Liberation Project—Statement and Bill of Rights." In *Rough times*, ed. by J. Agel. New York Ballantine, 1973. (Also included in *Radical Psychology, ed. by Phil Brown.)*

b) The North American Conference on Human Rights and Psychiatric Oppression

The North American Conference on Human Rights and Psychiatric Oppression has met annually since June 1973. The first Conference was held in Detroit, and was mainly organized by a group of "mental health" professionals. Since the organizers realized they needed to have at the conference some of the people whose rights were going to be discussed, they contacted the Mental Patients Liberation Project (MPLP) in New York City. The original title suggested by the organizers was something like "National Conference on the Rights of the Mentally Disabled" but was changed to its present title (except the North American part, which came in 1975) largely due to efforts of MPLP members. Around 200 people attended; they were mostly local and included ex-inmates, professionals, college students and professors. At this conference the ex-inmates were treated with great respect and the organizers seemed to have a real commitment to mental patients rights. The Detroit Conference established a pattern which has continued: that the Conference serve primarily as a means of joining together and exchanging ideas, rather than for any "hard" organizing.

The Second Conference (Topeka, 1974) is somewhat legendary. There was an exceptionally mellow feeling of unity among participants, who included both ex-inmates and professionals. The tradition of holding a demonstration at a local psychiatric institution began at this conference when 75 people marched to Topeka State Hospital.

The Third Conference (San Francisco, 1975) was initially dominated by large numbers of hip professionals ("radical therapists") who treated ex-inmates present in a contemptuous and patronizing way. Sharp clashes between the two groups followed. By the last day, the shrinks had been pretty much driven off, and a resolution was passed that the next year's conference would be open (for the first two days) only to ex-inmates and non-inmates already active in the anti-psychiatry movement.

The next conference (Boston, 1976) saw the ex-inmates firmly in control. This Fourth Conference generated some significant contributions to the anti-psychiatry movement's political analysis: in particular, the *Semantics Workshop* concentrated on developing a new language of self-definition which moves away from psychiatric terminology and into plain English that is consistent with the movement's ideology (see Appendix A: Anti-Psychiatry Glossary, based on this language), and a position paper, which is reprinted below.

The Fifth Annual Conference was held in Los Angeles. It held a wide variety of workshops and was responsible for the decision to hold the November 5, 1977 nation-wide day of protest against psychosurgery.

Bryn Mawr College, near Philadelphia, was the site of the 1978 Sixth Conference.

Detailed accounts of each Conference are available in various movement publications listed below. Back issues are generally available (see XI-e, Periodicals).

Articles on Detroit MP Conference. *Rough Times* 3(8), 1973.

Articles on the Fourth Conference on Human Rights and Psychiatric Oppresion. *RT: A Journal of Radical Therapy* 5(3), 1976.

Budd, Su, Collins, Jenny, Harris, Bob and Walker, Dianne. "The Boston Conference: four personal accounts." *Madness Network News* 4 (1) 1976.

Budd, Su, Stanley, Richard, Zinman, Sally L. and Jude. "The L.A. Conference: four personal accounts." *Madness Network News* 4 (5) Winter, 1978.

Burghard, Shirley, Chamberlin, Judi, Conference Women's Caucus, Goldberg, Joan, and Hudson, Wade. Articles on the Conference on Human Rights and Psychiatric Oppression in San Francisco, 1975. *Madness Network News* 3 (3) 1976.

Crazy David. "And in Los Angeles." *State and Mind* 6 (2) Winter, 1977.

Mills, Bruce. "NAPA Conference in L.A." *In A Nutshell* 5(4), September 1977.

Personal account of experiences at the Fifth Annual Conference.

Movement Notes. *Madness Network News*.

Column. Provides up-to-date information about Conference planning activities and meeting reports.

NAPA Newsletter.

This periodical bulletin is a good source of information about Conference-related news, planning, etc. See XI-e, Periodicals.

North American Conference on Human Rights and Psychiatric Oppression. "Demands." *Madness Network News* 4 (1) October, 1976.

"Statement of Conference on Human Rights and Psychiatric Oppression." Intro. by Sheila Koren. *State and Mind* 5(4), Nov.-Dec., 1976.

Concise summary of issues related to development of anti-psychiatry movement's new language; describes work of Semantics Workshop, one of the four workshops where the position paper was produced at the Fourth Conference. Includes a revised (non-official) version of the position paper, emphasizing semantic issues and changes. *State and Mind* said that they hope to do a fuller exploration of psychiatric terminology and the movement's response to it in a future issue.

Weitz, Don. Report on the Topeka Conference on Psychiatric Oppression. *Madness Network News* 2(5), 1974.

i) Position Paper of the Fourth Annual North American Conference on Human Rights and Psychiatric Oppression, 1976

This official version was endorsed by the Fourth Annual Conference at its final session and appeared in the Fall 1976 issue of the Mental Health Law Project Newsletter:

We support the abolition of all forms of involuntary psychiatric interventions, including but not limited to involuntary civil commitment, forced psychiatric procedures and "voluntary" procedures administered without informed consent. We oppose involuntary commitment and other forced psychiatric procedures on the following legal, moral, medical and humanitarian grounds:

they are unconstitutional – a denial of autonomy, personal freedom and and the due process requirements of the Constitution;

they are a form of preventive detention;

morally, they are reprehensible; scientifically, they are indefensible.

We affirm the right of all people to have an absolute right to control their souls, bodies and minds, as long as they do not infringe upon the rights of others.

We condemn the use of forced psychiatric procedures, such as drugging, shock, psychosurgery, restraints, seclusions and aversive behavior modification for the following reasons:

they cause suffering and injury which is often permanent; they are destructive and immobilizing and they are at best quackery (attempts to "cure" nonexistent diseases) and at worst torture (brutal, painful techniques to control human thought, feeling and conduct).

We oppose the institutional psychiatric system for many reasons:

it is inherently punitive, corrupt, oppressive and stigmatizing;

through its use of the "medical model" of human conduct, it invalidates varieties of human experience by calling them "mental illness" and it uses the trappings of medicine and science to mask the social-control function it serves;

it creates an extra-legal parallel police force which suppresses cultural and political dissidence;

it punishes individuals who have had or claim to have had spiritual experiences and invalidates those experiences by defining them as "symptoms" of "mental illness";

it feeds on the poor and the powerless: the elderly, women, children, sexual minorities, Third World people, and it creates a group of people who are dependent, stigmatized and easily manipulated;

it discredits the real needs of poor people by offering social welfare under the guise of psychiatric "care and treatment";

it creates environments (in the form of so-called hospitals and clinics) that rob people of their freedom, creativity and self-respect;

it distracts from social problems by treating individuals as if their difficulties were evidence of personal pathology rather than a reflection of the stresses and faults in society; it is a tool used not for personal or social enlightenment, but for maintaining the political, economic and social status quo.

We condemn the use of the words "mental illness," "mentally handicapped," "mentally disabled" and other psychiatric labels because they are stigmatizing and demeaning as well as unscientific and superstitious. We propose that nonmedical language be substituted whenever possible in order to demystify psychiatry, for example, psychiatric institution in place of "mental hospital," drug for "medication" and psychiatric procedure for "treatment."

We believe in the right of people to commit suicide. Dangerousness to self should never be used as a justification for incarcerating anyone.

We believe that real "help" can never be coercive.

We believe that so-called dangerous or assaultive people should be dealt with through the courts with due process and not through the psychiatric system. No one shall be locked up, ever, unless found guilty of committing a crime. We oppose the use of psychiatry in prisons and support all efforts to reform the criminal justice system.

The psychiatric system, whenever it functions, is harmful to the interests of people. Fundamentally tyrannical, it uses state power to enforce certain standards of conduct by punishing nonconformity with what is euphemistically called "treatment." Many are caught up in the system who don't want assistance of any kind and merely wish to be let alone. Assistance, when it is sought, should be available. But it should not be imposed on people through the psychiatric, or any other, system. As one possibility, we envision and are beginning to develop a network of small, voluntary support groups where the type and degree of assistance is decided upon by the people seeking the services themselves. We are also aware of the fact that many of the problems facing people today are rooted in the social system. Clearly, the time is ripe for creative change within society at large, and we are working toward that end as well.

So long as the psychiatric system exercises its illegitimate authority, our progress will be slow. But we shall not be deterred. We who have experienced the inhumanity of this system are joining together to expose its abuses and eliminate its power and to establish a truly just and free society. We invite everyone to join us in this struggle.

c) The European Network for Alternatives to Psychiatry

In Europe, the movement against psychiatric oppression has found a continental expression in the European Network for Alternatives to Psychiatry, formed in Brussels in 1974. It functions primarily as an information exchange network, bringing together for purposes of analysis and strategical planning various groups concerned with psychiatric oppression: mental patients groups, radical mental health workers (the network is committed to establishing some sort of liason between the two groups), and mental health lawyers. Involved in the Network are such well-known figures as Franco Basalgia and Giovanni Jervis (from Italy's *Psychiatria Democratica*), Laing and Cooper (England), Felix Guattari (France), and Mony Elkaim (Belgium). Fundamental to the Network's strategy is to work with other movements around the *depsychiatrization* of the problem of "madness'; like the North American movement, they offer a critique of society as a whole.

Conreur, Yves-Luc, Caster, Robert and Elkaim, Mony. "Trieste: selected statements." *State and Mind* 6 (2) (Winter 1977): 14-17.

Lovell, Anne. "Breaking the circuit of control." *State and Mind* 6 (2) (Winter 1977): 7-13.

A report on the Network's 3rd Conference in Trieste, Italy, including background information and analysis of underlying themes.

Seem, Mark. "International Network formed." *State and Mind* 5 (5) (March/April 1977): 11.

News analysis of European Network formation in January 1975. Describes activities and political perspective of one of the network's most active movement groups, the G.I.A. (Group of Information on Asylums) in Belgium.

Seem, Mark. "Update on the European Network." *State and Mind* 5 (6) June/July, 1977.

". . .Guattari summed up the general goal of the European Network from his own perspective thus: if the movements involved attack only the large-scale, visible structures and techniques of repression (on the macro-political level) — such as the psychiatric hospital, drugging, shock, etc. — the 'softer, kinder' (micro-political) techniques will be granted a more human status. Is it less dangerous. . . for someone severely depressed to enter into a long psychotherapy, than to change their living situation or take some medical 'treatment'? In other words, we can see repressive use made of drugs, shock seclusion, etc., but this does not necessarily mean that the non-visible verbal and non-verbal techniques (the 'therapeutic look' of approval or disapproval, screenings, the use of certain terminology and diagnoses, the 'free' associations, etc.) are less material or less effective in crushing not only a person's madness, anger, depression, etc. but also their energy, desires and capacities for radical transformation.

X SOME ALTERNATIVES TO INSTITUTIONAL PSYCHIATRY

Writings that discuss setting up anti-psychiatry alternatives to conventional therapy; reports on some alternative therapy institutions that have come into being. For feminist alternatives, see VII-d, Feminist Therapy.

a) Classic Experiments in Anti-Psychiatry

Barnes, Mary and Berke, Joseph. *Mary Barnes: two accounts of a journey through madness.* Middlesex: Penguin, 1973.

This work contains elaborate descriptions of Kingsley Hall. See I-a, Autobiographical Accounts.

Clark, Ted and Jaffe, Dennis T. "Change within a counter-cultural crisis intervention centre." In *Going crazy: the radical therapy of R.D. Laing and others,* ed. by H.M. Ruitenbeek. New York: Bantam, 1972.

Cooper, David. *Psychiatry and anti-psychiatry.* London: Granada/Paladin, 1970.

Cooper's book includes chapters reporting his Villa-21 anti-psychiatry experiment. See II-a-i, The British School: Writings and Interviews.

"The debate over Kingsley Hall." *Intellectual Digest* 2(1) (September 1971): 56-9.

"Two observers argue the validity of this communal test of R.D. Laing's theory of anti-psychiatry: sanctuary for the clinically oppressed or 'crash pad for crazies'." In "A Visit to Kingsley Hall" Albert Goldman argues against it. Morton Schatzman ("Madness and Morals", reprinted from *Counter Culture,* ed. by J. Berke) argues in its favor.

Friedrich, Otto. *Going crazy: an inquiry into madness in our time.* New York: Simon & Schuster, 1975.

This book discusses Kingsley Hall, sometimes poking fun at the R.D. Laing cult. See XI-a, General Works.

Glaser, Kristin and Gendlin, Eugene. "Main themes in Changes, a therapeutic community." *Rough Times* 3(6) (1973): 2-4.

Gordon, James S. "Who is mad? Who is sane? R.D. Laing in search of a new psychiatry." In *Going crazy: the radical therapy of R.D. Laing and others,* ed. by H. M. Ruitenbeek. New York: Bantam, 1972.

Gordon was a visitor to Kingsley Hall. See II-a-ii, The British School: Criticism and Reviews.

Jaffe, Dennis. "Number Nine: creating a counter institution." In *The Radical Therapist,* ed. by J. Agel. New York: Ballantine, 1973.

"Number Nine was created in October 1969 as a service for young people in crisis. It was founded by a group of young people who found the frustrations and internal contradictions of working within the existing mental health system too great."

Jaffe, Dennis T. and Clark, Ted. *Number Nine: autobiography of an alternate counselling service.* New York: Harper & Row, 1975.

This book is a revised edition of *Toward a Radical Therapy,* 1973.

Laing, R.D. "Metanoia: some experiences at Kingsley Hall, London." In *Going crazy: the radical therapy of R.D. Laing and others*, ed. by H.M. Ruitenbeek. New York: Bantam, 1972.

Mebane-Francescato, Donata and Jones, Susan. "Radical psychiatry in Italy: love is not enough." In *Rough Times,* ed. by J. Agel. New York: Ballantine, 1973.

About a radical therapeutic community set up in an Italian mental hospital under the guidance of Franco Basaglia.

Schatzman, Morton. "Madness and Morals." In *Counter Culture: the creation of an alternative society,* ed. by J. Berke. London: Peter Owen/Fire Books, 1969. (Also included in *R.D. Laing and anti-psychiatry,* ed. by R. Boyers and R. Orrill, and reprinted in adapted form in *The radical therapist,* ed. by J. Agel.)

British anti-psychiatrist Schatzman discusses the Philadelphia Association, which is affiliated with several self-governing households for ex-mental patients in Britain. His article centers mainly around Kingsley Hall, the largest of these households.

b) The Vancouver Mental Patients Association

The Vancouver Mental Patients Association (M.P.A.) began in 1971 when a group of ex-mental patients decided that if they wanted effective, relevant back-up help in the community they would have to do it themselves. Starting without any funds, M.P.A. has grown into a large government-funded project, and now owns and operates two apartment buildings, five residential houses, and Drop-In Centre.

M.P.A. runs on the principles of self-help and self-government (participatory democracy), and utilizes the philosophy of *power-reversal*, which means that the membership has the decision-making power—the power to hire and fire, to allocate funds, and to plan programs. This system is seen as essential to improving decision-making abilities and people's sense of self-worth. By contrast, the psychiatric treatment system based on the medical model offers little or no learning experiences relevant to promoting self-help and self-direction; rather, it perpetuates the self-defeating notion of incompetence.

M.P.A. activities range from social and recreational programs to patient advocacy, publication of a newsletter, public speaking, and producing literature and videotapes that promote M.P.A.'s philosophy. Criticism and self-criticism are an integral part of the M.P.A. program. Residences are run autonomously, and members can be voted out for failure to comply with M.P.A. regulations.

As a service organization, M.P.A. has been highly successful: for example, readmission rates to hospital for people involved in residence programs are about 10%, compared to 60% for the general population.

M.P.A., as a political organization, has been a mixed success. While spurts of political activity have led to some visible improvements (especially in areas of patient advocacy), there has been a failure to raise the political consciousness among the membership at large. Political activism has tended to be focused in a few individuals, with others giving approval without any practical support. The problem has many sources: in part, reliance on government funding has dulled M.P.A.'s political edge; many people coming to M.P.A. arrive fresh from a psychiatric institution where they have been taught that they are useless and weak (in addition, many are still being drugged with tranquilizers which tend to produce *enormous* apathy); and the Drop-In Centre's legendary policy of tolerance has had the effect of supporting a lot of "cop-out" behavior. Sexism has been a serious ongoing problem in residences and at the Drop-In Centre, and has been challenged, with limited success, by various women's groups within M.P.A. which have sprung up specifically to confront the issue.

M.P.A. is definitely not for everybody, but it has given many of us a space to begin getting our heads together.

Where applicable, copies are available by writing to: Mental Patients Association, 2146 Yew Street, Vancouver, B.C. V6K 3G7, Canada.

Beckman, Lanny. "M.P.A. is not for everybody." *In A Nutshell: Vancouver Mental Patients Association Newsletter* (11) February 7, 1972.

Documents M.P.A.'s transition from its early anarchism to the adoption of participatory democracy, where a few basic rules became necessary to serve the good of the community. Copies of this articles available at cost from M.P.A.

Beckman, Lanny. "Organizing a mental patients association," *Rough Times* 3(7) 1973.

M.P.A.'s founder describes some practical lessons learned along the way. For more of Beckman's writings, see VI, Professionalism & the Mental Health Industry.

Canadian Broadcasting Corporation. *Vancouver Mental Patients Association Videotape.* See XI-d, Audio-Visual.

Chamberlain, Judi. *On our own: patient-controlled alternatives to the mental health system.* New York: Hawthorn Books, 1978. "Inside the Mental Patients Association" Chapter.

This excellent chapter takes a perceptive and critical look at M.P.A. and its operations, examining what has happened to M.P.A. since it began in 1971. Asks some dis-comforting questions about the role of paid co-ordinators and non-patients in M.P.A., pointing out how the high proportion of non-patient co-ordinators has brought about a reduction of patient control over the organization.

Frank, K. Portland. *M.P.A. yesterday and today.* Unpublished essay, February 1977. 15 pages. Copies available for $1.50 plus self-addressed and stamped envelope from author, c/o Press Gang.

A much longer version of the introduction preceeding this section. Two-thirds of this paper is devoted to analyzing the history of M.P.A.'s sexism and (lack of) political consciousness.

Hooper, Jackie. *M.P.A. – a new direction for mental patients.* January 1976. (10 pages)

Statement by M.P.A. member. Copies available at cost from M.P.A.

In a Nutshell: Mental Patients Association Newsletter. See XI-e, Periodicals.

Martin, Bonnie, ed. *Head on.* Vancouver Mental Patients Association, 1978.

A handbook written by M.P.A. members. Includes: history of M.P.A., a "how-to" section on setting up your own self-help organization, reprints from old *Nutshells,* a section on organizational structure and its impact on mental health, poetry, prose, graphics, and more.

Mental Patients Association. *Homemade Videopackage.* See XI-d, Audio-Visual.

Mental Patients Association. *Madness unmasked.* See XI-b, Anthologies.

M.P.A. Revised Mental Health Act, 1973. (12 pages)

Put together by M.P.A. Research Committee following two years of extensive research and data gathering all over North America and Europe. Many of its ideas (e.g. the review panel system of patient advocacy) were incorporated into the revised British Columbia Mental Health Act of 1973 by the New Democratic Party government; others yet remain to be implemented by B.C.'s mental health legislation – a system which continues to neglect spelling out even the most basic rights of persons confined in mental hospitals. Copies available at cost from M.P.A.

National Film Board. *Vancouver Mental Patients Association.* Film. See XI-d, Audio-Visual.

Phillips, Frances, Hooper, Jackie, Batten, Cathy et al. "The Vancouver Mental Patients Association – the practical application of power reversal and self-help – a new concept of mental health in the community." Paper submitted to: Eighth Banff International Conference on Behaviour Modification, March 21-25, 1976.

This is the definitive paper on M.P.A. It was presented at the 1976 Banff Conference, where the participation of M.P.A. and the Vancouver Women's Health Collective marked the first time that "self-help" groups were invited to make presentations at this prestigious conference of leading professionals. For copies write: Weight Watchers Inc., 800 Community Drive, Manhasset, New York 11030, U.S.A.

Vancouver Mental Patients Association. Pamphlet.

Put together by the CBC in the wake of its "Man Alive" television show, about M.P.A. This ten page pamphlet is essentially a shorter version of the Phillips et al. Banff 1976 Conference paper. Available at cost from M.P.A.

Vancouver Mental Patients Association Society. *Constitution and By-Laws.* (3 pages)

Outlines in point form the objectives of M.P.A., and its operation. Defines members, their rights and duties. Gives regulations concerning meetings, voting, officers, books, financial statements, etc. Copies available at cost from M.P.A.

Vancouver Resources Society for the Physically Disabled. *Group home manual.* Handicapped Resource Centre, 1975.

This group adopted the M.P.A. model of communal living, with residents in charge of their own affairs. Copies available for $1.00 from: Handicapped Resource Centre, 8185 Main St., Vancouver, B.C. V5X 3L2, Canada.

c) Halfway Houses

Elizabeth Stone House. See VII-d, Feminist Therapy.

Jaffe, Dennis T. "A halfway house community." In *Going crazy: the radical therapy of R.D. Laing and others,* ed. by H.M. Ruitenbeek. New York: Bantam, 1972.

Describes the New Haven Halfway House, founded in 1967 by a group of Yale undergraduates as co-operative living arrangement for a coalition of students and people recently discharged from mental hospitals.

Rausch, H.L. & Rausch, C.L. *The halfway house movement: a search for sanity.* New York: Appleton-Century-Crofts, 1968.

An early classic study of halfway houses.

Rog, Dennis J. and Rausch, Harold L. "The psychiatric halfway house: how is it measuring up?" *Community Mental Health Journal* 11(2) 1975.

Two professionals examine 26 statistical reports on the effectiveness of the psychiatric halfway house. Results indicate that a median of approximately 80% of residents adjust to community living, and data suggest that rehospitalization rates are lower after stay in a halfway house.

Tomlinson, Peter B. and Cumming, John. "Coast Foundation Apartment Project." *Canada's Mental Health* 24(1) (March 1976): 23-8.

Describes a small apartment block for ex-mental patients which opened in Vancouver in 1974 as an alternative to the psychiatric boarding home system, which is overcrowded, restrictive and perpetuates dependency. Includes bibliography.

d) Berkeley Radical Psychiatry

Berkeley Radical Psychiatry (or Therapy) had its roots in Transactional Analysis. Formerly a student of Eric Berne, Claude Steiner has been one of its key theoreticians. Radical Therapy has also been shaped by input from feminism, largely under the influence of Hogie Wyckoff.

During the early 1970's, when the American Radical Therapy movement began, the Berkeley group was loosely identified with the Radical Therapist/Rough Times Collective and published some of its writing in *RT*. By the end of 1973, however, connections were severed over political differences and *RT* published a statement that it did not support the "apolitical orientation" of the Berkeley Center.

Radical Psychiatry sees conventional psychiatry as useless because it keeps people mystified about the true causes of their oppression, and also opposes it because the practice of psychiatry has been usurped and monopolized by the medical profession, who often uses it as a tool for furthering oppression. Consequently, the Berkeley School believes that "soul healing" must be returned to its non-medical origins, that it is best practiced in groups, and that its purpose is to assist people in becoming aware of the roots of their internalized oppression and combatting them.

Issues in Radical Therapy (IRT), its official journal, began publication in 1973. Presently, this school operates mainly through *IRT* and the Bay Area Radical Therapy Collective (see Appendix B-a, Mental Patients Rights/Anti-psychiatry Groups); their affiliates have also begun spreading in some areas of the U.S.

Although this school's operations are not based upon political activism, Radical Psychiatry does offer an essentially non-oppressive system of therapy to help people rout out internalized oppression and raise their political consciousness.

Issues in Radical Therapy (IRT).

See XI-c, Periodicals.

Lyons, Gracie. *Constructive criticism: a handbook.* Oakland: IRT Press, 1976.

Applies Maoist principles for solving personal and political problems within collective groups.

Steiner, Claude. "Guiding principles of a community RaP Center." In *Toward social change: a handbook for those who will,* ed. by R. Buckhout et al. New York: Harper & Row, 1971.

Describes theory and practice of the Berkeley Radical Psychiatry RaP Center.

Steiner, Claude M. "Radical psychiatry manifesto." In *The radical therapist,* ed. by J. Agel. New York: Ballantine, 1971.

Steiner, Claude M. "Radical psychiatry: principles." In *The radical therapist,* ed. by J. Agel. New York: Ballantine, 1971.

Steiner, Claude. *Games alcoholics play: the analysis of life scripts.* New York: Grove Press, 1971.

A description of the concepts of contact, permission and protection within the theoretical framework of Transactional Analysis as developed by psychiatrist Eric Berne.

Steiner, Claude. "The stroke economy." *Transactional Analysis Journal* 1(3) 1971.

". . . people's submission to their early basic training in relation to the exchange of strokes produces a population of stroke hungry persons who spend most of their waking hours procuring strokes; they are therefore frequently manipulated by persons who control the strokes through a monopoly of them." Steiner argues that the freeing up and equalizing of strokes is a key to therapy.

Steiner, Claude. *Scripts people live: transactional analysis of life scripts.* New York: Bantam, 1975.

About T.A. theory and script analysis. Largely concerned with Banal and Trap Scripts and how to get out of them. Two sections were contributed by Hogie Wyckoff, which deal with sex-role scripting for men and women.

Steiner, Claude et al., eds. *Readings in radical psychiatry.* See XI-b, Anthologies.

Steiner, Claude & Kerr, Carmen, eds. *Beyond games and scripts.* Oakland: IRT Press, 1976.

Annotated Eric Berne reader, selected from his complete works. Includes commentaries, annotated bibliography, T.A. glossary, and short biography of Eric Berne.

Wyckoff, Hogie, ed. *Love, therapy, and politics:issues in radical therapy — the first year.* See XI-b, Anthologies.

Wyckoff, Hogie. *Solving women's problems: through awareness, action, and contact.* See VII-d, Feminist Therapy.

e) Alternatives: General and Misc.

Action Magazine. See XI-e, Periodicals.

Chamberlin, Judi. *On our own: patient-controlled alternatives to the mental health system.* New York: Hawthorn Press, 1978.

Written by prominent ex-inmate activist. Has been geared towards general public. Chamberlin identifies three basic models of alternative facilities: 1) the partnership model, run by professionals and non-professionals, where "service recipients" don't make major decisions; 2) the supportive model, such as Vancouver Mental Patients Association, where non-patients and ex-patients are equals, and all the basic decision-making power belongs to those the facility serves; and 3) the separatist model, which excludes non-patients. Includes an account of Chamberlin's own psychiatric history and discusses the liberating effect of joining the psychiatric inmates' movement.

"Co-counselling – a do it yourself therapy: Parts 1 and 2." *Heavy Daze* (5) & (6).

Goldner, Virginia. "The politics of mental health in China." *State and Mind* 6(3) Spring 1978.

Describes how the Chinese use a very holistic approach to "mental illness," combining herbal medicine, acupuncture, political study, criticism/self criticism, productive labor and community support.

Gregory, Dick. *Natural diet for folks who eat: cookin' with Mother Nature.* New York: Harper & Row.

An introduction to natural healing.

Hermes, Jeanette. "On radical therapy." In *Going crazy: the radical therapy of R.D. Laing and others,* ed. by H.M. Ruitenbeek. New York: Bantam, 1972.

Jackins, Harvey. *Fundamentals of co-counselling manual*. Available from: Rational Island Publishers, P.O. Box 2081, Main Office Station, Seattle, Washington 98111, U.S.A.

Jackins, Harvey. *The human side of human beings: the theory of re-evaluation counselling*. Available from: Rational Island Publishers, P.O. Box 2081, Main Office Station, Seattle, Wa. 98111, USA.

Jaffe, Dennis T., ed. *In search of a therapy: personal accounts of the training, change, and growth of nonconventional therapists.* See XI-b, Anthologies.

Kunnes, Richard. "How to be a radical therapist." In *The radical therapist,* ed. by J. Agel. New York: Ballantine, 1971.

Kunnes, Richard. "Stealing mental health: theory and practice." In *The radical therapist,* ed. by J. Agel. New York: Ballantine, 1971.

San Francisco Bay Area U.S.-China Friendship Association. "Mental health in China." In *Rough times,* ed. by J. Agel. New York: Ballantine, 1973.

Based on psychologist Alan Wasserman's visit to China. Documents how the present Chinese mental health system serves the people. Describes current practices: no locks on doors, lobotomies and electroshock have been outlawed, no heavy drugging, group therapy and political study programs, community participation in helping patients – which includes welcoming them back home, etc. Relates mental health statistics which show that China's system has better success rate than North America's.

XI ANTI-PSYCHIATRY: GENERAL AND MISC. RESOURCE MATERIALS

a) General Works

This brief section includes works of a general or eclectic nature which do not fall into categories of present classification scheme.

Barnett, Michael. *People, not psychiatry: a human alternative to conventional psychotherapy.* (new ed.) Chicago: Regnery, 1975.

Brown, Phil. *Toward a Marxist psychology.* New York: Harper & Row, 1974.

Brown was trained as a psychologist and worked as an early member of the RT Collective. In this exploratory work, he examines relationships between class structure, capitalism, and the mental health industry. Includes criticisms of Szasz, Laing, Reich, Fanon, and other theorists. Discusses present role and activities of mental patients' liberation movement and feminist theory.

Deleuze, Gilles & Guattari, Felix. *Anti-Oedipus: capitalism and schizophrenia.* Translated by Robert Hurley, Mark Seem & Helen R. Lane. New York: Viking Press/Richard Seaver Books, 1977.

A book that pushes beyond attempts to synthesize Marx and Freud, *Anti-Oedipus* sets out to track down the traces of fascism. Preface by Michel Foucault.

Friedrich, Otto. *Going crazy: an inquiry into madness in our time.* New York: Simon & Schuster, 1975.

Journalistic survey of madness: historical documents, case histories, current practices, interviews with mental patients, etc. Includes discussion of Laing and Kingsley Hall with somewhat critical view. Concludes that his research only reinforced his initial prejudice against psychiatry, both traditional and new varieties like Laing's, and that madness is not romantic.

Henley, Nancy. *Body politics.* Englewood Cliffs, New Jersey: Prentice-Hall, 1977.

A study of non-verbal communication and power, it both demystifies and entertains. Exposes how "masculine" and "feminine" gestures reinforce men's control over women. Henley is a *State and Mind* anti-psychiatry writer of long standing.

Jackson, Don D. *Myths of madness.* New York: Macmillan, 1964.

"L'Antipsychiatrie." *La Nef* (42) Janvier-Mai 1971.

La Nef is a cultural periodical. This whole issue was devoted to anti-psychiatry, with submissions from important writers of the French anti-psychiatry movement (P.C. Racamier, Robert LeFort, Michel Gribinski, Andre Bourgignon, and others).

Mannoni, Maud. *Le psychiatry, son "fou" et la psychoanalyste: la question de l'anti-psychiatrie.* Paris: Editions du Seuil, 1970.

A classic text of the French anti-psychiatry movement.

McLeester, Dick. *Welcome to the magic theater: a handbook for exploring dreams.* Available for $3 (plus 30¢ postage) from: Food for Thought, P.O. Box 331, Amherst, Ma. 01002, U.S.A.

Shows how to use dreams as a vehicle for social change. Includes annotated bibliography plus sections on "Consciousness-Raising and Social Change" and "On Spiritual and Therapeutic Tyranny".

Nuttall, Jeff. *Bomb culture.* London: MacGibbon & Kee, 1968.

Discusses Laing, Berke, Kingsley Hall, the Free U Movement, and other counter-cultural activities of the 1960's; includes discussion of Laing's association with "Sigma", a London-based avant-garde precursor of the counter-cultural Underground.

Racamier, P.C. *Le psychoanalyste sans divan.* Paris: Payot, 1970.

A classic text of the French anti-psychiatry movement.

Schneider, Michael. *Neurosis and civilization: a Marxist/Freudian synthesis.* Translated by Michael Roloff. New York: Seabury Press, 1975.

Attempts to link "mental illness" with the commodity exchange nature of capitalism. Includes discussion of the Socialist Patients Collective (S.P.K.), a Marxist anti-psychiatry group in Heidelberg, West Germany. This book is quite academic and heavily colored by Schneider's psychiatric training.

Scull, Andrew T. *Decarceration – community treatment and the deviant: a radical view.* Englewood Cliffs, New Jersey: Prentice-Hall, 1977.

Examines the politics behind letting loose psychiatric and other inmates. Argues that the alleged "humane" rationale used for dumping these people on the streets is a fake. Exposes capitalist economics behind decarceration programs in terms of social control expenses.

b) Anthologies

Some of the following anthologies are devoted entirely to anti-psychiatry; others cover a broader range of topics. Most anthology titles have also been cross-referenced in other sections where they specifically apply. Most lists of articles are not all-inclusive, but serve to identify a representative cross-section or especially important documents.

Agel, Jerome, ed. *The radical therapist.* New York: Ballantine, 1971. (Currently out of print, but the *State & Mind* Collective is trying to get Ballantine to publish more.)

Anthology of writings selected from the best of *RT*'s first year of publication. This and the second *RT* anthology (*Rough Times*) make excellent reading about the development of the radical psychology/counter therapy movement.

For further information about the journal's current activities, see XI-e, Periodicals, *State & Mind.* Some of *RT*'s classic articles can also be obtained individually: see XI-c, Pamphlets for listing of new *RT* reprint pamphlets now available.

Includes: "Radical Psychiatry: Principles" (Claude Steiner); "Radical Psychiatry and Movement Groups" (Claude Steiner); "How to be a Radical Therapist" (Rick Kunnes); "Radical Therapy Needs Revolutionary Theory" (Terry Kupers); "Flection/Reflection" (Mary Barnes); "Madness and Morals" (Morton Schatzman); "Anti-Psychiatry" (Interview with Joe Berke); "Brainwashing and Women" (a Redstockings Sister); "The Myth of the Vaginal Orgasm" (Anne Koedt); "Letter to her Psychiatrist" (Nadine Miller); "Oedipus and Male Supremacy" (Robert Seidenberg); "The Personal is Political" (Carol Hanisch); "Is Women's Liberation a Therapy Group?" (Marilyn Zweig); "Marriage and Psychotherapy" (Phyllis Chesler); "Radical Psychiatry in Women's Groups" (Hogie Wyckoff); "Community Mental Health as Pacification Program" (Jim Statman); "Number Nine: Creating a Counter Institution" (Dennis Jaffe); "Rights of Children" (Summary recommendations of the Workshop on the Rights of Children, Berkeley Conference, Revolutionary Peoples Constitutional Convention, Nov. 14-15, 1970); "Gay Liberation Manifesto" (Carl Wittman); "Radical Psychiatry Manifesto" (Claude Steiner); "Editorials from *The Radical Therapist*."

Agel, Jerome, ed. *Rough times.* New York: Ballantine, 1973.

Writings selected from *RT*'s second year of publication. "RT feels the sense of total revolution much more sharply than before. . . We changed the name from *The Radical Therapist* to *Rough Times* since the original title was misleading – radical is a term used by too many people who don't want to 'rock the boat' . . . . Rip-off types were springing up all over, calling themselves 'radical therapists' . . . We are focusing on providing news and communication between groups involved in organizing and struggle. . . . the women's movement, the anti-imperialist movement, and in many areas. . . ."

Includes: "Ordeal in a Mental Hospital" (Anonymous); "Social Change at Harrowdale State Hospital: Impression I" (Cynthia Ganung); "Social Change at Harrowdale State Hospital: Impression II" (Phil Brown); Radical Psychiatry in Italy: 'Love is Not Enough' " (Donna Mebane-Franscescato & Susan Jones); "Mental Health in China" (San Francisco Bay Area U.S.-China Friendship Association); "On Professionalism" (Michel L. Glenn); "Detherapizing Society" (Rick Kunnes); "Psychology as a Social Problem: An Investigation into the Society for the Psychological Study of Social Issues" (Lanny Beckman); "Union Organizing" (Marlene Cohen); "In Defence of Individual Therapy" (Tim de Chenne); "Suggestions for Working with Heavy Strangers and Friends" (Kristin Glaser); "People's Psychiatry Sheet 1: Handling Psychiatric Emergencies" (Michael Glenn); "People's Psychiatry Sheet 2: Common Drug Emergencies" (Chuck Robinson); "Psychiatry and Homosexuality: New 'Cures' " (Louis Landerson/Liberation News Service); "Race, Class, and the I.Q. Controversy" (Richard Bickley); "Lobotomies are Back" (Liberation News Service); "Vacaville: Lobotomies, Shock Therapy, and Torture for 'Violent' California Prisoners" (Good Times/Liberation News

Service); "Civilization and Its Dispossessed: Wilhelm Reich's Correlation of Sexual and Political Repression" (Phil Brown); "Back in the USSR: the Politics of Psychiatry" (Nancy Henley); "Vietnam: A Feminist Analysis" (Boston Lesbian Feminists).

Berke, Joseph, ed. *Counter culture: the creation of an alternative society.* London: Peter Owen/Fire Books, 1969.

A selection of essays and graphics describing several counter-cultural institutions (mainly U.S.) and political viewpoints identified with them which were active around the late 1960's.

Includes: "The Creation of an Alternative Society" (Joseph Berke); "Cultural Revolution - U.S.A. 1968" (R.G. Davis) "Kommune 1 Visited" (Joseph Berke); "Consciousness and Practical Action" (Allen Ginsberg); "You Had Better Come On Home" (Stokely Carmichael); "Strasbourg 1966" (Basic Document); "Applications of Ecstasy" (Jeff Nuttall); "The Free University of New York" (Joseph Berke); "Madness and Morals" (Morton Schatzman); "The Diggers" (David Mairowitz); "The Post-Competitive, Comparative Game of a Free City" (Basic Document); "Fuck the System" (Basic Document); "Free London" (Basic Document).

Block, N.J. & Dworkin, Gerald, eds. *The I.Q. controversy: critical readings.* New York: Random House/Pantheon, 1976.

A reader of essays by leading authorities on alleged genetic differences in "racial" intelligence. These writings disclose the political rather than scientific content of the I.Q. controversy. Contains older literature as well as debates around newly published works (e.g. Jensen's and Herrnstein's racist I.Q. theories).

Boyers, Robert and Orrill, Robert, eds. *R.D. Laing and anti-psychiatry.* New York: Harper & Row, 1971.

A collection of much of the serious writing which has been addressed to Laing and the views with which he is usually identified. These writings speak both for and against Laing. "At least one selection indicates the variety of mis-uses to which Laing can be put. . . one must suppose, it is as culture critic, a new species of the psychiatrist as prophet, that Laing would be known. . . ."

Includes: "R.D. Laing: Self, Symptom & Society" (Peter Sedgwick); "The Meta-Journey of R.D. Laing" (Jan B. Gordon); "Schizophrenia and the Mad Psychotherapist" (Leslie H. Farber); "Laing's Models of Madness" (Miriam Siegler, Humphrey Osmond & Harriet Mann); "An Interview with Dr. Theodore Lidz" ; "An R.D. Laing Symposium with R. Coles, L. Farber, E. Friedenberg, K. Lux"; "Madness and Morals" (Morton Schatzman); "An Interview with Dr. Joseph Berke"; "Flection/Reflection" (Mary Barnes); "Afterword: A Medium with a Message: R.D. Laing" (Benjamin Nelson).

Brown, Phil, ed. *Radical psychology.* New York: Harper & Row, 1973.

A reader which "synthesizes the currents of thought and action from Marx to the present which involve the struggle to end psychological and all other forms of oppression." Put together by the RT Collective.

Includes: General introduction and section introductions by Phil Brown; Marx on consciousness and alienation; Fanon on "mental health is revolution"; Reich on sexual-political liberation; Laing on the mystification of experience; Cooper on the death of the family; Mary Barnes on the 'schizophrenic voyage'; Naomi Weisstein on sexism in psychology; Mental Patients Liberation on action against psychiatric atrocities; Szasz on the myth of mental illness; personal experiences of oppressive therapy; original articles on the Marx/Freud synthesis.

Buckhout, Robert and 81 Concerned Berkeley Students, eds. *Toward social change: a handbook for those who will.* New York: Harper & Row, 1971.

Compiled by an undergraduate course in Social Problems. Topics covered are: Black / Chicano / Asian-American / Native-American /White consciousness; violence; the social sciences; professionalism, Naderism; alienation; alternative life styles; the drug scene; encounter groups; population control; education; and discussions of the meaning and possibility of social change. This book's great flaw is that it includes no section on women.

Cooper, David, ed. *To free a nation: the dialectics of liberation.* Middlesex: Penguin, 1968.

Contains some of the principal addresses delivered at The Congress on the Dialectics of Liberation held in London at the Roundhouse in Chalk Farm from 15 July to 30 July 1967. This Congress was organized by four psychiatrist-leaders of the British Anti-psychiatry movement (R.D. Laing, David Cooper, Joseph Berke, and Leon Redler). "This book is centrally concerned with the analysis destruction – destruction in two senses: firstly, the self-destruction of the human species by racism (Carmichael), by greed (Gerassi on Imperialism), by the erosion of our ecological context (Bateson, Goodman), by blind, frightened repression of natural instinctuality (Marcuse), by illusion and mystification (Laing and myself); secondly, closely interwoven with the first sense, these essays study the human conditions under which men destroy each other (Jules Henry's essay on "Psychological Preparation for War" in particular explored this subject). So it is a book about mass suicide and mass murder and we have to achieve at least a minimal clarity about the 'mechanisms' by which these processes operate before we begin to talk about liberation."

Cox, Sue, ed. *Female psychology: the emerging self.* Chicago: Science Research Associates, 1976.

Feminist reader of essays on female psychology. Contains articles by Bart, Chesler, Koedt, Weisstein, Radicalesbians, Mead, and others.

Garskoff, Michele H., ed. *Roles women play: readings towards women's liberation.* Belmont, Ca.: Wadsworth/Brooks-Cole, 1971.

Twelve feminist readings on women and psychology.

Glenn, Michael, ed. *Voices from the asylum.* New York: Harper & Row, 1974.

Anthology of writings by mental patients; presents day-to-day oppression happening in mental institutions today. Also includes sections on mental patients' liberation groups.

Gornick, Vivian & Moran, Barbara K., eds. *Woman in sexist society: studies in power and powerlessness.* New York: New American Library/Signet, 1972.

Important feminist reader, contains current writings by 31 women scholars and activists. Several articles are relevant to women and psychology.

Includes: "The paradox of the Happy Marriage" (Jessie Bernard); "Depression in Middle-Aged Women" (Pauline B. Bart); "Psychology Constructs the Female" (Naomi Weisstein); "Ambivalence: The Socialization of Women" (Judith M. Bardwick & Elizabeth Douvan); "Patient and Patriarch: Women in the Psychotherapeutic Relationship" (Phyllis Chesler); and "The Compassion Trap" (Margaret Adams).

Hamalian, Leo & Karl, Frederick, eds. *The fourth world: the imprisoned, the poor, the sick, the elderly and underaged in America.* New York: Dell, 1976.

These diverse articles are about the countless people who have been "dumped" into invisibility. They describe a "sub-nation" within a larger nation which amounts to more than one-quarter of the population.

Includes: "A Day in Folsom Prison" (Eldridge Cleaver); "Recent Letters and an Autobiography" (George Jackson); "Women in Cages" (Jessica Mitford); "Emerging American Indian Politics: The Problem of Powerlessness" (Joyotpaul & Jean Chaudhuri); "Someday Us Poor Is Going to Overrule" (Shirley Dalton); "Welfare Mothers Speak Out"; "Uncle Tom and Tiny Tim: Some Reflections on the Cripple as Negro" (Leonard Kriegel); "The Mentally Retarded: Society's Hansels and Gretels" (Benjamin & Dorothea Braginsky); "The Insanity Bit" (Seymour Krim); "Dump Therapy" (Marilyn Becker); "Insane Liberation Front"; "Introduction to *The Coming of Age*" (Simone de Beauvoir); "Juvenile Courts, Family Courts, and The Poor Man" (Monrad Paulsen).

Hirsch, Sherry, Adams, Joe Kennedy et al., eds. *Madness Network News reader.* San Francisco: Glide Publications, 1974.

A selection from articles, poems, graphics, and letters that have appeared in *MNN* plus new material. Gives information about psychiatric institutions, treatments, the embryonic movement to change the system, and correspondence from readers and members of the madness network. See also XI-e, Periodicals, *Madness Network News.*

Huber, Joan, ed. *Changing women in a changing society.* Chicago: University of Chicago Press, 1973.

Originally a special issue of *The American Journal of Sociology.* Presents 21 scholarly studies in sociology, mostly by women well known in the field.

Documents and evaluates recent changes due to impact of women's movement on various groups and areas of life. Includes article on "Adult Sex Roles and Mental Illness".

Jaffe, Dennis T., ed. *In search of a therapy: personal accounts of the training, change, and growth of nonconventional therapists.* New York: Harper & Row/Harper Colophon, 1975.

Eleven "statements from a group of therapists. . . trying to move from a personal critique of therapy as a social institution towards new ways of helping people."

Includes: "Psychiatric Miseducation" (James S. Gordon); "The Mythology of Professionalism and an Emerging Alternate Role" (Ted Clark); "The Healer, the Community, or the Bureaucrat" (Dennis T. Jaffe); "I Did It – Scribbles on a Notebook Wall" (Joan M. Constantine); "The Uses of Madness" (James S. Gordon).

Kaplan, Bert, ed. *The inner world of mental illness: a series of first person accounts of what it was like.* New York: Harper & Row, 1964.

This reader gives excellent inside glimpses of madness and its "treatment". Contains large number of excerpts from the madness literature classics, as well as personal documents by less famous mental patients. Several of these cases have been studied by such writers as Laing, Szasz, Schatzman, Silverman, and Freud.

Includes: "Living with Schizophrenia" (Norma McDonald); "I Am Crazy Wild This Minute. How Can I Learn to Think Straight?" (Lara Jefferson); "The Universe of Bliss and the Universe of Horror: A Description of a Manic-Depressive Psychosis" (John Custance); "The Insanity Bit" (Seymour Krim); "A Little-Known Country" (Anton Boisen); "Paranoia" (Daniel Paul Schreber); "Excerpt from *A Mind that Found Itself*" (Clifford Beers); "Excerpt from *Autobiography of a Schizophrenic Girl*" (Marguerite Sechehaye); "Through the Looking Glass" (Mary Cecil); "Excerpt from *Narrative of the Treatment Experienced by a Gentleman During a State of Mental Derangement*" (John Perceval); "A Suicide Diary" (R.S. Cavan); "Epilepsy" (Margiad Evans); "The Doctors Do Not Understand My Illness" (Vaslav Nijinsky); "The Nausea Has Not Left Me and I Don't Believe It Will.... It Is No Longer an Illness or a Passing Fit: It Is I" (Jean-Paul Sartre); "I Swear, Gentlemen, That to Be Too Conscious Is An Illness – A Real Thoroughgoing Illness" (Fyodor Dostoevsky).

Levin, Hannah, ed. *Handbook on the politics of mental health.* New York: Marcel Dekker, 1978.

McCaffrey, Joseph A., ed. *The homosexual dialectic.* Englewood Cliffs, New Jersey: Prentice-Hall, 1972.

Compilation of articles representing a broad cross-section of views about homosexuality. Presents both straight and radical gay perspectives. Only 2 of its 15 articles pertain to lesbians.

Mental Patients Association. *Madness unmasked.* Vancouver: Mental Patients Publishing Project, 1974. Available for $2 from: Mental Patients Association, 2146 Yew St., Vancouver, B.C. V6K 3G7, Canada.

MPA's creative writing book. A wide-ranging compilation of poetry, graphics, and prose written primarily by ex-mental patients who are MPA members. It chronicles personal experiences of being labelled "mentally ill", struggles against varieties of psychiatric oppression and against the patriarchal machine, as well as break-through and revolution. Excellent introduction gives brief history of MPA and the publishing project.

Miller, Jean Baker, ed. *Psychoanalysis and women.* Middlesex: Penguin, 1973.

Sixteen eminent psychoanalysts (Karen Horney, Alfred Adler, Clara Thompson, Gregory Zilboorg, Mary Jane Sherfey, and others) attack Freud's phallocentric view and revise the traditional psychoanalytical approach to women. Includes Horney's pioneer work: "The Flight from Womanhood: The Masculinity Complex as Viewed by Women and Men".

Millman, Marcia & Kanter, Rosabeth Moss, eds. *Another voice: feminist perspectives on social life and social science.* Garden City, New York: Doubleday/Anchor, 1975.

This compilation of essays examines sociology critically to see how knowledge of the social world can be expanded to consider those formerly invisible realities that have now been made visible by the women's movement.

Includes: "Women and Medical Sociology: Invisible Professionals and Ubiquitous Patients" (Judith Lorber); "Black Women and Self-Esteem" (Lena Wright Myers); "She Did It All for Love: A Feminist View of the Sociology of Deviance" (Marcia Millman); "The Sociology of Feeling and Emotion: Selected Possibilities" (Arlie Russell Hochschild); "Feminist Perspectives in Sociological Research" (Arlene Kaplan Daniels).

Morgan, Robin, ed. *Sisterhood is powerful: an anthology of writings from the women's liberation movement.* New York: Random House/Vintage, 1970.

Important feminist reader, the first comprehensive collection of writings from the women's movement. Contains writings on Third World women, lesbians, the psychological and sexual repression of women, and many other areas.

Includes: " 'Kinde, Kuche, Kirche' As Scientific Law: Psychology Constructs the Female" (Naomi Weisstein); "A Theory of Female Sexuality" (Mary Jane Sherfey); "A Psychiatrist's View: Images of Women – Past and Present, Overt and Obscured" (Natalie Shainess); "Notes of a Radical Lesbian" (Martha Shelly).

Price, Richard H. & Denner, Bruce, eds. *The making of a mental patient.* New York: Holt, Rinehart & Winston, 1973.

Radical Therapist / Rough Times Collective, eds. *The radical therapist.* Middlesex: Penguin, 1974. Available in U.K., Australia, New Zealand, and Canada.

This collection of articles for an English public combines the best from *RT's* first two U.S. books, *The Radical Therapist* and *Rough Times.* Includes *RT's* classic articles on Radical Therapy, professionalism, hospitals and treatments, sexism, children, mental patients' liberation, self-help, and communities.

Ruitenbeek, Hendrik M., ed. *Going crazy: the radical therapy of R.D. Laing and others.* New York: Bantam, 1972.

Compilation of several important documents from both British Anti-Psychiatry and American Radical Therapy movements, plus a few critical articles addressed to Laing. Begins with informative seven page introduction by Ruitenbeek, explaining the origins and general political/theoretical orientation of each School.

Includes: "Letter to the Medical Directors of Lunatic Asylums" (Antonin Artaud); "Metanoia: Some Experiences at Kingsley Hall, London" (R.D. Laing); "On Radical Therapy" (Jeanette Hermes); "The Other Shore of Therapy" (David Cooper); "Anti-psychiatry: Interview with Joe Berke" (Andrew Rossabi); "Interview with David Cooper"; "Who is Mad? Who is Sane? R.D. Laing in Search of a New Psychiatry" (James S. Gordon); "Flection/Reflection" (Mary Barnes); "The Obvious" (R.D. Laing); "R.D. Laing: Psychiatry and Apocalypse" (David Martin); "R.D. Laing and the Young" (Hendrik M Ruitenbeek); "Psychotherapy – A Medical Procedure?" (J.S. Werry); "Oedipus Rex: Tragedy or Strategy?" (Robert Seidenberg); "Mental Health in a Corrupt Society" (Lester A. Gelb); "Change Within a Counter-Cultural Crisis Intervention Centre" (Ted Clark & Dennis T. Jaffe); "Kinder, Kuche, Kirche" (Naomi Weisstein); "A Halfway-House Community" (Dennis T. Jaffe); "The Accursed Race" (Robert Seidenberg); "Sara's Odyssey – Acid and the Youth Culture" (Dennis & Yvonne Jaffe); "Radical Psychiatry" (Claude M. Steiner).

Scheff, Thomas J., ed. *Mental illness and social processes.* New York: Harper & Row, 1967.

Representative thinking and research of the 1960's on "societal reaction to mental disorder". Employing the anthropological model, these studies seek to describe the "behavior of members of society with respect to illness without necessarily sharing the assumptions that are made in that society about illness" and consequently, they lead to the recognition of some of the blind spots inherent in the medical model.

Includes: "Some Factors in Identifying and Defining Mental Illness" (David Mechanic); "The Psychological Meaning of Mental Illness in the Family" (Marian Radke Yarrow, Charlotte Green Schwartz, Harriet S. Murphy & Leila Calhoun Deasy); "The Mental Health of the Hutterites" (Joseph W. Eaton & Robert J. Weil); "The Illusion of Due Process in Commitment Proceedings" (Luis Kutner); "Social Conditions for Rationality: How Urban and Rural Courts Deal with the Mentally Ill" (Thomas J. Scheff); "Psychiatric and Social Attributes as Predictors of Case Outcome in Mental Hospitalization" (Simon Dinitz, Mark Lefton, Shirley Angrist & Benjamin Pasamanick); "The Abbots" (R.D. Laing & A. Esterson); "A Review of

Sanity, Madness, and the Family" (John K. Wing); "Some Factors Influencing the Development and Containment of Psychiatric Symptoms" (Jules V. Coleman); "The Obligation to Remain Sick" (Ben Bursten & Rose D'Esopo); "Institutionalism in Mental Hospitals" (John K. Wing); "The Myth of Mental Illness" (Thomas S. Szasz); "Normal Deviants" (Erving Goffman); "Paranoia and the Dynamics of Exclusion" (Edwin M. Lemert); "Notes on the Sociology of Deviance" (Kai T. Erikson).

Scheff, Thomas J., ed. *Labeling madness.* Englewood Cliffs, N.J.: Prentice-Hall/Spectrum, 1975.

Ten essays which discuss more recent developments in the "labeling theory" of mental illness. Part I contains statements of "the need for change in conceptualizing and dealing with madness in our society." Part II looks at possible solutions.

Includes: "Schizophrenia as Ideology" (Thomas J. Scheff); "On Reason and Sanity: Some Political Implications of Psychiatric Thought" (Thomas J. Scheff); "Suggestion Effects in Psychiatric Diagnosis" (Maurice K. Temerlin); "On Being Sane in Insane Places" (David L. Rosenhan); "Paranoia or Persecution: The Case of Schreber" (Morton Schatzman); "Mental Diseases in China and Their Treatment" (Ruth Sidel); "The Idiom of Demonic Possession" (Gananath Obeysekere).

Steiner, Claude, ed. *Readings in radical psychiatry.* New York: Grove Press, 1975.

Book of seminal writings which first appeared in the "Berkeley Issue" of *The Radical Therapist.* Covers: Radical Psychiatry theory, therapy, principles, manifesto; women; community organizing; and resumé of early criticisms of Radical Psychiatry. Contains writings by Claude Steiner, Hogie Wyckoff, Daniel Goldstine, Peter Lariviere, Robert Schwebel, Joy Marcus, and members of the Radical Psychiatry Center.

Smith, Dorothy E. & David, Sara J., eds. *Women look at psychiatry.* Vancouver: Press Gang, 1975.

A feminist reader "of articles written by women who are or have been involved with psychiatry, either professionally or as patients or both. . . . a critical book, concerned with how psychiatry has contributed to women's oppression, and with ways of changing that. Its aim is to make visible how current psychiatric practice affects women, and to offer readers a chance to learn from women's experiences in doing it differently".

Includes: "Women and Psychiatry" (Dorothy E. Smith); "How the Psychiatric Profession Views Women" (Elinore L. King); "Women's Oppression and Psychiatric Oppression" (Judi Chamberlin); "It Was an Eighteenth Century Horror Show!" (as told to Marsha Enomoto); "Struggling To Be Born" (Judi Chamberlin); "Shrink! Shrank! Shriek!" (Barbara Findlay); "The Statistics on Mental Illness: What They Will Not Tell Us About Women and Why" (Dorothy E. Smith); "Women, Sex Role Stereotypes, and Mental Health: Catch 22" (Meredith Kimball);" 'Female Neurosis': A Valid Protest"

(Eve-Lynne Rubin); "Feminist Counselling: A Perspective" (Alison Griffith); 'A Feminist Therapy Session" (Rita MacDonald & Dorothy Smith); "Becoming a Non-Sexist Therapist" (Sara David); "Emotional Self-Defense Groups for Women" (Sara David); "I'm Not Crazy After All" (Barbara Joyce).

Szasz, Thomas S., ed. *The age of madness: the history of involuntary mental hospitalization presented in selected texts.* Garden City, New York: Doubleday/Anchor, 1973.

". . . a wide variety of documents written by a great many men and women – physicians, journalists, attendants, and patients; famous and unknown; Americans, Russians, Frenchmen, and others; living and dead."

Includes: "Observations on Psychiatric Confinement" (Daniel Defoe, Sir John Fortesque-Aland & John Conolly); "The Utility of Public Asylums for Lunatics" (Philippe Pinel); "Deception and Terror as Cures for Madness" (Benjamin Rush); "A Lunatic's Protest" (John Perceval); "Madness and Blackness" (*The American Journal of Insanity,* 1840); "Democracy as Mental Disease" (*The American Journal of Insanity,* 1851); " 'In Case You Refuse. . . .' " (from the Records of Dorothea Dix Hospital, Raleigh, N.C.); "Madness and Marriage" (E.P.W. Packard); "Expert Testimony in Judicial Proceedings" (John Ordronaux); "The Psychiatric Assassination of King Ludwig II of Bavaria" (Werner Richter); "The Commitment of Bishop Morehouse" (Jack London); "From the Slaughterhouse to the Madhouse" (Ugo Cerletti); "The Discovery of Lobotomy" (Egas Moniz); "The Sick and the Mad" (Frigyes Karinthy). " 'Patient Labour' in the British Mental Hospital System" (J.A.R. Bickford); "Illegitimacy and Insanity" (*The Guardian*); 'Psychiatric Justice in Canada" (Harvey Currell, Peter Bruton & Sidney Katz, from the *Toronto Daily Star* and the *Toronto Telegram*); "Position Statement on the Medical Treatment of the Mentally Ill" (the American Psychiatric Association and the National Association for Mental Health); "The Moral Career of the Mental Patient" (Erving Goffman); "Adjustment to the Total Institution" (Byron G. Wells); "The Insanity Bit" (Seymour Krim); "The Machine in Ward Eleven" (Charles Willeford); "Sanity Through Suffocation" (*Medical World News*); "Johnny Panic and the Bible of Dreams" (Sylvia Plath).

Wyckoff, Hogie, ed. *Love, therapy, and politics: Issues in Radical Therapy – the first year.* New York: Grove Press, 1976.

Reprints of 20 best articles from 1973, *IRT*'s first year. Covers: Radical Therapy, theory and practice; women and men; Transactional Analysis; fat liberation; high school misfits; and other issues.

Weitz, Don, ed. Forthcoming anthology of autobiographical accounts of patients' experiences in Canadian mental hospitals. For more information, write: Don Weitz, P.O. Box 7251, Station A, Toronto, Ontario, Canada.

c) Pamphlets/Catalogues/Misc. Publications

This section lists pamphlets and other miscellaneous publications of a general anti-psychiatry nature; many others have been listed in the specific section where they best apply. Check in journals such as *Heavy Daze, Madness Network News,* and *State and Mind* for the latest publications. For addresses not listed below, see Appendix B, Directory.

A bibliography of materials useful for change in mental hospitals. No. 533 and 534, 1974. Available from: Council of Planning Librarians, Box 229, Monticello, Ill. 61856, U.S.A.

Boston MPLF. *Our journal.* 40 pages. Available for $1.50 from: Mental Patients Liberation Front.

A collection of news, poetry, personal stories and information.

Castles in the air. EPOC Pamphlet No. 2. Produced by Galactic Services, July 1976. Available for 30p from: EPOC Collective.

A critique of the recent Government white paper (Better Services for the Mentally Ill October 1975). Includes brief anti-psychiatry directory (England).

Chamberlin, Judi. *Consciousness-raising.* Available from: Alliance for the Liberation of Mental Patients.

Reprinted from the December 1975 issue of *Madness Network News,* this article analyzes the potential value of consciousness-raising groups for ex-mental patients.

Citizen participation in mental health: a bibliography. 15 pages. No. 559, 1974. Available from: Council of Planning Librarians, P.O. Box 229, Monticello, Ill. 61856, U.S.A.

Includes both conventional and radical references.

Field, Ellen. *The white shirts: an indictment of psychiatric oppression.* Write to: 14531 Oval Road, Irvine, Ca. 92705, U.S.A.

Hawaii diary. Available for $2.50 from: Psychiatric Inmates Solidarity Movement, Hawaii Chapter.

Hess, Nancy. *Nutly 77.* Write to: Nancy Hess, 7025 Woolston Road, Philadelphia, Pa. 19138, U.S.A.

Recently updated comprehensive guide to services available to ex-patients re-entering society in the Philadelphia area. Compiled by ex-mental patient. Covers jobs, educational resources, self-help programs, and community centers.

How to cope with the Mental Health Act 1959. EPOC Pamphlet No. 1. First Edition, Jan. 1975. Available from: EPOC Collective.

A practical survival manual, dealing specifically with England and Wales. Includes legal information, an appendix on psychiatric drugs, group directory for some anti-psychiatry alternatives, and more.

IRT Press. Write to: P.O. Box 32544, Oakland, Ca. 94623, U.S.A.

Vital reading and listening materials on radical psychiatry, feminist writings, community organizing, mental health movement, other current writings. Mail order list is free upon request.

KNOW, Inc. P.O. Box 86031, Pittsburgh, Pa. 15221, U.S.A.

Catalogue available which lists their many reprints, pamphlets, etc. on feminist topics. Much of their material deals with women and psychiatry/psychology. See also VII, Psychiatry & Women for listings of several KNOW publications.

LAMP information packet. Copies of their most recent packet available for donations of at least $4 from: Center for the Study of Legal Authority and Mental Patient Status.

Introduction to a range of the key legal and structural issues involved in working for fundamental reform of present "mental health" system. Covers: inmate rights; enforcement of statutory rights provisions; case law; court decisions; psychosurgery, shock procedures, the right to refuse treatment; a "streetsheet" for California residents (June 1974); updates dealing with AB4481 and AB1032; a critique of the "right to treatment"; a discussion of conservatorship; nonmedical alternatives to institutionalization; sex-based discrimination against women; a discussion of the rights of persons under 18 years of age; and more.

Organizing for health care: a tool for change. Source Catalog No. 3. Available for $5.95 from: Organizer's Book Center, P.O. Box 21066, Washington, D.C. 20009, U.S.A.

Published in 1974 by Beacon Press; part of a series of organizers' catalogues. Includes 30 page section on Mental Health, listing books, pamphlets, films, tapes, and organizations. Covers mental patients support groups, techniques of psychiatric abuse, feminist counselling, alternatives to institutionalization, crisis centers, legal advocacy, community mental health services, Third World, and occupational health.

Psychiatry as social control: an annotated bibliography. 8 pages. By Jenny, Orion & Thuna. Available for $.50 from: Network Against Psychiatric Assault, San Francisco.

Poetry book. Available for $2 from: Psychiatric Inmates Solidarity Movement, Hawaii Chapter.

RT new reprint series. Pamphlets. Available for $.50 each or $.40 for any nine or more from: RT, Inc., P.O. Box 89, West Somerville, Ma. 02144, U.S.A.

The following titles offer reprints of some of the great *RT* classics, both new and old: #1 *Mental patients liberation;* #2 *Weapons of the psychiatric establishment;* #3 *Women's sexuality;* #4 *The sexual abuse of children;* #5 *Psychoanalysis and the Menarche;* #6 *"Insanity" in mental asylums;* #7 *Social control in prisons;* #8 *Classism in therapy;* #9 *Feminist counselling.*

d) Audio-Visual

Anti-psychiatry, pro-patient film. Write to: Radical Film Project, Cambridge-Goddard, 5 Upland Road, Cambridge, Mass. 02140, U.S.A.

Asylum. Film. Distributed by: Vision Quest, P.O. Box 206, Lawrenceville, N.J. 08648, USA.

A documentary about R.D. Laing and life in one of his "blow-out centers" in London. Filmed by a crew who lived at Kingsley Hall for six weeks.

Critical mass gallery. Videotape. Write to: Bob Sandidge, Audio Visual Services, Elgin State Hospital, 750 S. State Street, Elgin, Ill. 60120, U.S.A.

Loan copies available in several videotape types. This videotape deals with some of the oppressive aspects of institutional psychiatry and mental "health". A major flaw, however, is the tape's failure to confront institutional psychiatry on deeper levels.

Dialectics of liberation records. Can be ordered from: The Institute of Phenomenological Studies, 1 Sherwood Street, London W1, England.

Presentations from David Cooper's book, *The Dialectics of Liberation* (see XI-b, Anthologies) and other major discussions at the Congress are available as 12" longplay records.

Includes: DL3—"Beyond Words" (David Cooper); DL4—"Obvious" (R.D. Laing); DL5—"Politics and Psychotherapy of Mini and Micro Groups" (Ross Speck); DL13 & DL14—Two record set of open discussion which included David Cooper, Ronald Laing, Stokely Carmichael, and Allen Ginsberg.

Do no harm. Film. For distribution, contact: Grim Films, P O. Box 1811, San Francisco, Ca. 94101, U.S.A.

"CAUTION! The American Drug Industry may be hazardous to your health." This 42-minute color film is a documentary exposing the questionable advertising and sales practices of the American pharmaceutical industry.

Drug ad slides. Available on two week loan from: Gretchen Muller, Feminist Studies, Cambridge-Goddard Graduate School, 1878 Massachusetts Avenue, Cambridge, Mass. 02140, U.S.A.

A collection of slides from ads in medical and psychiatric journals. They point out contradictions between profit and ethics, and sex-role stereotyping of male and female "symptoms" which these drugs purport to cure.

Fountain house. Film. Available from: Indiana University Audio Visual Center, Bloomington, Ind. 47401, U.S.A.

This 29-minute film documents the operation of a halfway house in the "Hell's Kitchen" section of New York City.

The great Atlantic radio conspiracy radio program tapes. Available individually or by a series contract from: Howard Ehrlich, GARC, 2743 Maryland Avenue, Baltimore, Md. 21218, U.S.A.

Some tapes of special interest are: *Health Care in America; Politics of Mental Health I & II* (Two tapes, featuring members of Baltimore's Mental Patients Liberation Front, psychosurgery critic Peter Breggin, and *Rough Times* staff member, Nancy Henley); *Sexism; Gay Liberation; Women and Mental Health; Prisons.*

Hurry tomorrow. Film. Available in the United States from: Tri-Continental Film Center, 333 - 6th Avenue, New York, N.Y. 10014, U.S.A.; in Canada from: DEC Films, 121 Avenue Road, Toronto, Ont. M5R 2G3, Canada; in Australia and New Zealand from: Australian Film Institute, P.O. Box 165, Carlton South, Victoria, Australia 3053; and in Europe from: Contemporary Films Ltd., 55 Greek St., London, WIV 6DB, England.

This explosive 80-minute documentary was filmed on a psychiatric locked ward in Norwalk State Hospital in Los Angeles. "Earlier documentaries on conditions in mental hospitals raised a call for reform. *Hurry Tomorrow* shows a reformed ward, a sanitary, comfortable, enlightened ward. Hopefully it shows as well that reform is no answer, that the velvet gloved oppression of liberal psychiatry is really not much of an improvement over the iron fist of traditional psychiatry. The film makes clear that nothing short of radical change can lead to humane and acceptable alternatives to the present 'mental health' system." (from "Review" by Brian McCaffrey, *Madness Network News* 3(6) 1976).

NAPA tape. Available for $3.50 from: Network Against Psychiatric Assault, 558 Capp Street, San Francisco, Ca. 94110, U.S.A.

A 33-minute cassette tape featuring NAPA's historical Tribunal at the sleep-in at Gov. Brown's office, and Sandy Gordon, singing her composition, "Fight On, Ex-Patients, Fight On!"

Radio free madness. Ex-psychiatric inmate radio program in San Francisco area (KPFA, 94.1). Also distributed to St. Louis, Mo. and Fresno (KFCF, 88.1). For more information, write c/o Teish, Network Against Psychiatric Assault, 558 Capp Street, San Francisco, Ca. 94110, U.S.A.

State of mind. Film. Available through: Philadelphia Association, 74a Portland Road, London W11, England.

A film made by a New York film crew at a new residential community of the Philadelphia Association. It hopes to convey the mood of the people sharing their experiences and helping one another.

The titicut follies. Film. Available from: Grove Press Film Division, 196 W. Houston St., New York, N.Y. 10014, U.S.A.

85-minute documentary, filmed in the 1960's. An important precursor to *Hurry Tomorrow* which exposes psychiatric imprisonment in its cruder forms.

Vancouver Mental Patients Association homemade videopackage. Write to: Mental Patients Association, 2146 Yew Street, Vancouver, B.C. V6K 3G7, Canada.

This 45-minute videotape about M.P.A. was put together in 1975, largely through the efforts of M.P.A. member Dennis Blue. It covers all aspects of M.P.A. operation, activities, and philosophy. Available on loan for free, or for purchase at cost of reproduction (about $30 to $40).

Vancouver Mental Patients Association. Film. Available from: National Film Board, 1161 West Georgia Street, Vancouver, B.C., Canada.

This half-hour color film provides many excellent glimpses of day-to-day life at the drop-in centre and in the residences. Some parts nicely capture how M.P.A. people support and care for each other.

Vancouver Mental Patients Association. Videotape. Write to: Mr. Ian Chambers, International Relations and Export Officer, Canadian Broadcasting Corporation, Toronto, Ont., Canada.

This half-hour videotape was professionally made early in 1977 by the CBC for its "Man Alive" program. Much of this video is about the residence program, showing how the M.P.A. model works.

Video tapes by, for, and about mental patients. Information co-ordinator is Leon Rosenblatt, 333 East Fifth Street, New York, N.Y. 10003, U.S.A.

Some of these tapes emphasize reform and abolition of coercive psychiatry. They include personal experiences of ex-patient activists, poetry, music, drama, and interviews with Allen Ginsberg and ACLU lawyer, Bruce Ennis.

Wednesday's child. Film. (Also called *Family life*.) Available from: Cinema Five, 595 Madison Avenue, New York, N.Y. 10022, U.S.A.

A 108-minute film about Kingsley Hall in London.

e) Periodicals

The Abolitionist. American Association for the Abolition of Involuntary Mental Hospitalization, Inc. (A.A.A.I.M.H.), c/o Post Office, University of Santa Clara, Santa Clara, Ca. 95053, U.S.A.

Periodical devoted to changing present laws of involuntary mental hospitalization. Published by the group that Szasz helped found.

ACT/Action Magazine. c/o Ms. Shirley Burghard, B-1104 Ross Towers, 710 Lodi Street, Syracuse, N.Y. 13203, U.S.A.

"News, poetry, letters, practical suggestions, by ex-inmates and others struggling to free themselves from the hold of the medical establishment. Edited and published by a long-time anti-psychiatry activist. *Action* emphasizes self-help in its many aspects: self-healing through nutrition and vitamin alternatives to drugs, legal self-help, political organizing, feminism, Christianity, etc." (Mad Librarian, *MNN*). Published bi-monthly.

Alternative Press Index. Alternative Press Centre, Inc., P.O. Box 7229, Baltimore, Md. 21218, U.S.A.

This quarterly indexes material that appears in publications of its subscribing alternative presses. Many of the subject headings cover political issues and struggles. An excellent place to hunt for current news stories and articles pertaining to anti-psychiatry. *Madness Network News* and *State and Mind* are indexed here. Expensive to subscribe to, but found in most large libraries.

Arbours Network News. c/o Arbours Housing Association, 55 Dartmouth Park Road, London NW5, England.

Academically biased along the lines of Schatzman and Berke's thought.

Bar None. P.O. Box 124, W. Somerville, Ma. 02144, U.S.A.

Prison support paper.

Behavior Control Newsletter. c/o National Alliance Against Racist and Political Repression, 150 Fifth Avenue, Room 804, New York, N.Y. 10011, U.S.A.

Recently initiated by the Task Force Against Behavior Control and Human Experimentation as a tool in the struggle against behavior control programmes.

Benjamin Rush Society Newsletter. c/o F. Bartlett, 119 W. 87th Street, New York, N.Y. 10024, U.S.A.

Published by an organization devoted to studying the behavioural sciences from a Marxist viewpoint.

The Body Politic. Box 7289, Station A, Toronto, Ontario M5W 1X9, Canada.

A gay liberation journal dedicated to building gay movement and growth of gay consciousness. Contains feature articles and news stories. Published ten times yearly.

Canadian Association for the Abolition of Involuntary Mental Hospitalization Newsletter. Box 282, Whitby, Ont., Canada.

Published by the C.A.A.I.M.H., a group founded in 1972 on principles similar to those of the A.A.A.I.M.H. Available with a $5/year membership.

de Gekkenkrant. P.O. Box 3286, Amsterdam, Netherlands.

Publication (translated "The Lunaticspaper") which is largely circulated inside Dutch institutions. They are in contact with anti-psychiatry movement groups in Holland.

Guide to Alternative Periodicals. Sunspark Press, Box 6341-P, St. Pete Beach, Fl. 33736, U.S.A.

Contains information on over 400 magazines and journals concerned with alternative lifestyles. Available for $2.

Feminist Therapist Roster. c/o Annette Brodsky, Department of Psychology, University of Alabama, Box 6234, University, Ala. 35486, U.S.A.

Published at intervals by the Association for Women in Psychology. Lists name, address, phone number, training and experience, therapy services or interests, and a brief statement of therapist's position within range of feminist viewpoints. Feminist therapists who wish to be listed are asked to write to same address.

FPS: A Magazine of Young People's Liberation. Youth Liberation, 2007 Washtenaw Avenue, Ann Arbor, Mi. 48104, U.S.A.

Covers all aspects of youth liberation. Listed in the Alternative Press Index.

Gay People and Mental Health. Box 3592, Upper Nicollet Station, Minneapolis, Mn. 55403, U.S.A.

A monthly bulletin focusing on the oppression of gays by the mental health industry, and providing information on liberated methods of help/self-help for gays.

Heavy Daze. c/o EPOC, 111 Tavistock Crescent, London W1, England.

Anti-psychiatry journal and newsletter produced by people affiliated with COPE. Contains articles, news stories, poetry, cartoons, book reviews and lots of other good information. Strong psychiatric inmate bias. Includes a guide to alternatives in Britain, especially the London area.

Homosexual Counselling Journal. HCCC Inc., 30 East 60th Street, New York, N.Y. 10022, U.S.A.

Humpty Dumpty. 28 Redbourne Avenue, London N3, England.

Radical psychology magazine.

In A Nutshell: Mental Patients Association Newsletter. 2146 Yew Street, Vancouver, B.C. V6K 3G7, Canada.

Published several times yearly. Contains M.P.A. news, political articles, book reviews, accounts of members' experiences, poetry, graphics, and other information on patients' rights issues.

Idiot News. 2 Primrose Street, Lancaster, England.

Radical psychology magazine produced by a group of university psychology students.

Issues in Radical Therapy. The IRT Collective, P.O. Box 23544, Oakland, Ca. 94623, U.S.A.

Published four times yearly by the Berkeley Radical Psychiatry Center. A "practical political journal which serves as a forum for dialogue and exchange of information among people who are involved in the radical therapy movement." Contains many writings relevant to women. Listed in the Alternative Press Index.

Madness Network News, Inc. P.O. Box 684, San Francisco, Ca. 94101, U.S.A.

"All the Fits That's News to Print." Published about 6 times per year. This journal and *State and Mind* are currently the two best sources of current anti-psychiatry movement news and information. *MNN* has legally incorporated as an organization separate from, but allied with, Network Against Psychiatric Assault. As it evolved, *Madness* staff gradually became taken over by ex-psychiatric inmates. *Madness Network News Reader* is also available (see XI-b: Anthologies, Hirsch et al. for description). *Madness* is listed in the Alternative Press Index. A list of their back issues is available from *MNN.*

MPLF Newsletter. Mental Patients Liberation Front, Box 156, West Somerville, Ma. 02144, U.S.A.

Comes out several times a year. Send donation if possible.

MPU Newsletter. c/o Mental Patients Union, National Information Centre, 16 Clifton Gardens, St. Georges Road, Hull HU3 3QB, England.

NAPA Newsletter. Network Against Psychiatric Assault, 558 Capp Street, San Francisco, Ca. 94110, U S.A.

A listing of Bay Area meetings, demonstrations and events related to the struggle against psychiatry. Published bi-monthly.

Not So Patient Voice. c/o The Gathering Place, 7 N. Congress Street, Athens, Oh. 45701, U.S.A.

A newsletter for the expression of ideas of some former and present mental patients.

Rising Up Crazy. The Rising Up Crazy Collective, c/o Project Release, 4 West 76th Street, New York, N.Y. 10023, U.S.A.

Bi-monthly publication to serve the needs of the various ex-patient groups of the East Coast and Midwest. Has no official writing staff, but comprises a collection of writings from different groups. Includes reports on activities of various movement groups, legal issues, personal experiences, poetry, etc.

State and Mind. RT, Inc., P.O. Box 89, West Somerville, Ma. 02144, U S.A.

North America's oldest anti-psychiatry journal, whose original slogan was: "Therapy means change, not adjustment". Formerly called *RT: A Journal of Radical Therapy, Rough Times, The Radical Therapist.* Features political analyses of the mental health industry, feminist, gay, and prisoners' issues. Includes movement news, book reviews, and other up-to-date information about anti-psychiatry scene, especially U.S. East Coast. Published four times yearly. Back issues available; listed in each issue. See XI-b, Anthologies for anthologized *RT* material, and XI-c, Pamphlets for listing of *RT* Reprints and other material. *RT/State and Mind* is indexed in the Alternative Press Index.

Tightwire. P.O. Box 515, Kingston, Ont., Canada

Prison inmate's magazine whose purpose is to "dissolve the barriers of their physical imprisonment by sharing their attempts to free themselves from the mental bondages that engulf them".

Welcome Back. 3206 Prospect Avenue, Cleveland, Oh. 44115, U.S.A.

Newsletter and information exchange for people who have had mental hospitalization – a place to share their experiences of psychiatry.

Womanspirit. Box 263, Wolf Creek, Or. 97497, U.S.A.

Journal about feminist spirituality, women's culture, healing. Has forum for women doing ritual experiments. Quarterly.

Work Force. Vocations for Social Change, 5951 Canning Street, Oakland, Ca. 94609, U.S.A.

This resource magazine has special issues on madness, child care organizing, gay workers, community and more, including current job listings and resources for change.

f) Posters/Buttons/T-Shirts

Anti-forced drugging poster. Available from: Network Against Psychiatric Assault, 558 Capp Street, San Francisco, Ca. 94110, U.S.A

Designed by the San Francisco Poster Brigade. It is not for sale, but donations are requested. The poster should be publicly displayed. It says: "To Hell With Their Profits. Stop Forced Drugging of Psychiatric Inmates!"

I'm not mad I'm angry. Poster. Design by Pat Smith from the cover of *Women Look at Psychiatry.* Available for $1.50 from: Press Gang Publishers, 603 Powell Street, Vancouver, B.C. V6A 1H2, Canada.

Mental health is revolution. Poster by Judy Greenberg. Available for $1.00 from: RT, Inc., P.O. Box 89, West Somerville, Ma. 02144, U.S.A.

NAPA Poster & Button. Available for $.50 each from: Network Against Psychiatric Assault, 558 Capp Street, San Francisco, Ca. 94110, U.S.A.

Stop psychiatric drug pushing. Poster for the demonstration against Smith Kline & French pharmaceutical manufacturers (Thorazine, Stelazine, Parnate, Eskalith, etc.). Available for $1.00 from: The Alliance for the Liberation of Mental Patients, 112 S. 16th Street, #1305, Philadelphia, Pa. 19102, U.S.A.

T-Shirts. Available for $4 each from: Mississippi Mental Health Project, P.O. Box 951, Jackson, Ms. 39205, U.S.A.

Has large "Thorazine" on the front, and on the back it says "Free the Whitfield 3,000". Beige. Comes in small, medium, and large sizes.

APPENDIX A: TOWARD AN ANTI-PSYCHIATRY GLOSSARY

(Information Sources: Statement of 4th Conference on Human Rights and Psychiatric Oppression, with Introduction by Sheila Koren, *State and Mind* 5(4) Nov.-Dec. 1976, and conversations with Judi Chamberlin)

The anti-psychiatry movement, originally organized under the terminology of psychiatry, has now begun to develop a new language of self-definition based upon its political analysis. This development of a new terminology received a major thrust at the Semantics Workshop of the 4th North American Conference on Human Rights and Psychiatric Oppression (Boston, 1976). Psychiatric jargon, with its concepts of "patienthood" and "mental illness", has served to oppress and mystify the victims of psychiatry. The new language of anti-psychiatry, in contrast, exposes the social and emotional reality of the psychiatric system in plain English terms.

The following glossary briefly lists a few terms from the anti-psychiatry movement's new language.

Mentalism is the assumption that certain kinds of behavior are sane/normal, and that anything outside of these is crazy and requires psychiatric treatment; this viewpoint does not take into account the idea that there might be individual reasons for crazy behavior.

Sane Chauvinism has a similar meaning to Mentalism: that mental patients are oppressed by non-patients' attitudes towards them. As an oppressive force, it runs parallel to many others, such as racism, sexism, etc.

Some plain English terms as substitutes for psychiatric jargon:

Psychiatric Term	*Plain English*
Symptom	Characteristic, Trait
Behavior	Conduct
Medication	Drug
Chemotherapy	Drugging
Electrotherapy, Electrical Stimulation Therapy	Electroshock
Mental Health Professional (psychiatrist, psychologist, etc.)	Mental Illness Professional
Mental Health System	Mental Illness System
Mental Patient, Mentally Disabled, Mentally Handicapped Person	Psychiatric Inmate
Treatment, Therapy	Psychiatric Intervention
Treatment, Therapy	Psychiatric Procedure

APPENDIX B: DIRECTORY OF ANTI-PSYCHIATRY GROUPS AND RELATED ORGANIZATIONS

Since things are constantly changing, this list will be at least partially obsolete by the time you read it. More up-to-date information and news about both established and newly-forming groups can be found in *Madness Network News, State and Mind, Heavy Daze,* and various feminist, gay, prisoners', etc. publications. *Madness Network News* also provides a regular listing of contact persons: individuals interested in starting ex-inmate/anti-psychiatry groups, or user/patient-run alternatives to the psychiatric system.

It should be noted that not all of these groups share similar politics, and that not all of their politics are necessarily endorsed by the women at Press Gang Publishers.

To help me revise this list for the next edition of the Bibliography, please write (c/o Press Gang) and tell me about any groups that should be added on, or any changes of address. Any groups wishing me to include a brief description of themselves should send a blurb outlining who they are, what they do, etc. *Please write!*

a) Mental Patients Rights/Anti-Psychiatry Groups

i) Canada

Canadian Association for the Abolition of Involuntary Mental Hospitalization. Box 282, Whitby, Ont., Canada.

The C.A.A.I. M.H. was founded in 1972 on principles similar to the American Association for the Abolition of Involuntary Mental Hospitalization. It is run by a Board of Directors who are professionals. Membership is $5/year. The group publishes a newsletter. It believes that "persons who are presumed to be mentally ill are entitled to the same rights as any other Canadian citizen".

Coast Foundation Society. 876 East 18th Avenue, Vancouver, B.C., Canada.

Established in 1972 to provide recreation and activity programs for residents of Vancouver psychiatric boarding homes. Now operates a drop-in centre used by 200 or more persons, an apartment block housing 40 or more ex-psychiatric inmates, and a second apartment block opening soon. Also see X-c, Halfway House, Tomlinson & Cumming.

Mental Patients Association Society. 2146 Yew Street, Vancouver, B.C. V6K 3G7, Canada. See X-b, Vancouver Mental Patients Association.

Ontario Mental Patients' Association. c/o Box 7251, Station A, Toronto, Ont., Canada.

Project Release. 27 Victoria Street North, Kitchener, Ont., Canada.

ii) United States

ACT/Action. c/o Shirley Burghard, B 1104 Ross Towers, 710 Lodi Street, Syracuse, N.Y. 13203, U.S.A. See XI-e, Periodicals, Action Magazine.

Advocates for Freedom in Mental Health. 928 North 62nd Street, Kansas City, Ks. 66102, U.S.A.

Alliance for the Liberation of Mental Patients. 112 South 16th Street, Room 1305, Philadelphia, Pa. 19103, U.S.A.

They are working on a patients' rights manual for Pennsylvania institutions. Will soon be publishing a newsletter. Preliminary arrangements are underway for producing a "hard-hitting propaganda film" on the Mental Patients Liberation Movement. They ask people to send them money and ideas for their film.

American Association for the Abolition of Involuntary Mental Hospitalization (A.A.A.I.M.H.). c/o Post Office, University of Santa Clara, Santa Clara, Ca. 95053, U.S.A.

Founded by psychiatrist Thomas S. Szasz. Attempts to change medical opinion and mental health laws in order to curb the dangerous abuses of psychiatric power. The periodical, *The Abolitionist,* is its official publication.

Americans for Health Freedom. Box 862, Lawrence, Ks. 66044, U.S.A.

Ann Arbor Mental Patients Project. c/o Drug Help, 621 East Williams, Ann Arbor, Mi. 48104, U.S.A.

Another Alternative. 1316 North 42nd Street, Omaha, Ne; 68031, U.S.A.

Center for the Study of Legal Authority and Mental Patient Status (LAMP). Central Station, P.O. Box 3233, Hartford, Ct. 06103, U.S.A.

Research, legal and publicity group. Active at conferences on legal rights, and serves as an information center on patients' rights.

Center for the Study of Psychiatry. 4628 Chestnut Street, Bethesda, Md. 20014, U.S.A.

Center for the Study of Psychiatry. 1827 - 19th Street N.W., Washington, D.C. 20009, U.S.A.

Psychiatrist Peter Breggin's headquarters; does psychosurgery research and information distribution.

Citizens Against Shock. c/o Adamski, 1704 S.E. Taylor, Portland, Or. 97214, U.S.A.

Citizens' Commission on Human Rights. 1610 New Hampshire Avenue N.W., Washington, D.C. 20009, U.S.A.

Coalition Against Forced Treatment (CAFT). c/o Mental Health Consumer Concerns, Box 3742, Hayward, Ca. 94540, U.S.A.

CAFT has general meetings and committees, mainly in the Berkeley-Oakland area. Members are now also meeting to form a community of former psychiatric inmates, similar to Project Release in New York.

Coalition to Stop Institutional Violence. P.O. Box 89, West Somerville, Ma. 02144, U.S.A.

Committee Against Psychiatric Oppression. c/o Bill Hafling, S-68 Morrill Hall, University of Minnesota, Minneapolis, Minn. 55455, U.S.A.

Community Mental Health Legal Services of the Legal Aid Bureau. 341 North Coivert Street, Baltimore, Md. 21202, U.S.A.

Research, legal and publicity group.

Consumers of Mental Health Services. c/o Shaunee County Mental Health Association, 1268 Western, Topeka, Ks. 66604, U.S.A.

The Gathering Place. 7 N. Congress Street, Athens, Oh. 45701, U.S.A.

Insane Liberation Front. c/o T. Carwile, Rt. 4, Box 126, Walnut Hollow Road, Lynchburg, Va. 24503, U.S.A.

Institute for the Study of Medical Ethics. c/o Barbara Halstead or Jeanne Robinson, P.O. Box 17307, Los Angeles, Ca. 90017, U.S.A.

A nonprofit organization, established in 1974. Its purpose is to ensure the protection of patients regarding human experimentation and to firmly establish their rights under the law.

Issues in Radical Therapy (IRT). Box 23544, Oakland, Ca. 94623, U.S.A.

Contact point for Berkeley Radical Psychiatry. Also see X-d, Berkeley Radical Psychiatry.

LAMP. See Centre for the Study of Legal Authority and Medical Patient Status, above.

Madness Network News, Inc. Box 684, San Francisco, Ca. 94101, U.S.A. See XI-e, Periodicals.

Massachusetts Chapter of the Medical Committee for Human Rights. 1151 Massachusetts Avenue, Cambridge, Ma. 02138, U.S.A.

Does research into areas such as psychosurgery and compiles information for public distribution.

Mental Health Consumer Concerns of Alameda County (M.H.C.C.). Box 3742, Hayward, Ca. 94540, U.S.A.

Mental Health Law Project. 84 Fifth Avenue, New York, N.Y. 10011, U.S.A.

Mental Health Law Project. 1220 - 19th Street N.W., Suite 300, Washington, D.C. 10036, U.S.A.

Mental Patients Civil Liberties Project. 1315 Walnut Street, Suite 1600, Philadelphia, Pa. 19107, U.S.A.

Mental Patients Liberation Front. P.O. Box 156, West Somerville, Ma. 02144, U.S.A.

Now operating a drop-in center for ex-inmates. They are hoping to open a chapter in the North Shore area. See the essay in IX-a, Mental Patients' Liberation Fronts.

Mental Patients Liberation Project. c/o George Brewster, 3407 Wessynton Way, Alexandria, Va. 22309, U.S.A.

Mental Patients Liberation Project. 109 South Gilmor Street, Baltimore, Md. 21223, U.S.A.

Mental Patients Liberation Project. Box 15472, New Orleans, La. 70175, U.S.A.

Mental Patients Liberation Project. Box 1745, Philadelphia, Pa. 19105, U.S.A.

Mental Patients Liberation Project. c/o Mike Gallagher, 1626 S.E. 39th Avenue, Portland, Or. 97214, U.S.A.

Mental Patients Liberation Project. Box 158, Syracuse, N.Y. 13201, U.S.A.

Mental Patients Resistance. P.O. Box 185, Croton-on-Hudson, N.Y. 10520, U.S.A.

Mental Patients' Rights Association. c/o Sally Zinman, P.O. Box 301, Loxahatchee, Fl. 33470, U.S.A.

Network Against Psychiatric Abuse. c/o Ms. Jan McGrew, P.O. Box 162058, Sacramento, Ca. 95816, U.S.A.

Network Against Psychiatric Assault (NAPA). 558 Capp Street, San Francisco, Ca. 94110, U.S.A.

NAPA is "an organization dedicated to the elimination of involuntary commitment and forced psychiatric 'treatment' ". The San Francisco office is NAPA's mailing address.

Network Against Psychiatric Assault. c/o Carol Thompson, 512 W. Wilson Street, #307, Madison, Wi. 53703, U.S.A.

Network Against Psychiatric Assault. c/o Beattie, H-16 Koshland, U.C.S.C., Santa Cruz, Ca. 95064, U.S.A.

Network Against Psychiatric Assault. c/o Greg Berglund, 736 Santa Rita Place, San Diego, Ca. 92109, U.S.A.

Network Against Psychiatric Oppression. P.O. Box 667-F, New York, N.Y. 10010, U.S.A.

Patient Advocacy Legal Service. Washington University Law School, St. Louis, Mo. 63130, U.S.A.

Information clearinghouse in areas of patients' rights, especially mental commitment.

Patients Organized for Environmental Therapy (POET). NAPA Chapter, Box 7253, Imola, Ca. 94558, U.S.A.

Patients' Rights Organization. 1223 W. 6th St., Cleveland, Oh. 44113, U.S.A.

Active "in four main areas – living conditions of patients and housing for ex-patients; job discrimination against ex-patients; the general rights of ex-patients and patients; and community education regarding the public attitude toward the plight of emotional illness victims."

People's Rights Organization. 1347 South West Blvd., Apt. G, Rohnert Park, Ca. 94928, U.S.A.

Project Renaissance. c/o PRO, 8614 Euclid Avenue, Cleveland, Oh. 44106, U.S.A.

Project Release. 202 Riverside Drive, #4E, New York, N.Y. 10025, U.S.A.

Operates a community center and several "all the way houses" – communal apartments without staff where group members live and support one another. *Release* also does various other ex-inmate-run projects.

Psychiatric Inmates' Rights Collective (PIRC). P.O. Box 299, Santa Cruz, Ca. 95061.

A group dedicated to fighting for an end to forced treatment, and encouraging inmate-controlled alternatives.

Psychiatric Inmates' Solidarity Movement – Hawaii Chapter. P.O. Box 88228, Honolulu, Hi. 96815, U.S.A.

Rights Organization for Mental Patients. c/o Presbyterian-Methodist Center, 1112 - 19th Avenue, Nashville, Tn. 37212, U.S.A.

Scarlet Letter Group. c/o the Daily Planet, 1609 W. Grace Street, Richmond, Va. 23220, U.S.A

Smash Hospital Slavery – Begin at Keifer. Box 425, Fort Shelby Station, Detroit, Mi. 48231, U.S A.

State and Mind (RT, Inc.). P.O. Box 89, West Somerville, Ma. 02144, U.S.A. See XI-e, Periodicals.

Vermont Health Rights Committee. c/o Helvarg, 76 North Union Street, #6, Burlington, Vt. 05401, U S.A.

VIA/Life Project. c/o Lucia Gerbino Worley, 14 Washington Valley Road, Morristown, N.J. 07960, U.S.A.

Welcome Back. 3206 Prospect Avenue, Cleveland, Oh. 44115, U.S.A. See XI-e, Periodicals.

iii) International

European Anti-Psychiatry Network. Contact person: Felix Guattari, c/o Gardes Fous, 1 Rue des Fosses Saint-Jacques, Paris 75005, France.

This network was formed in January 1974 following an international conference on psychiatric oppression held in Brussels. The General Secretariat of the network is located at 39, avenue Louis Bertrand, Brussels, Belgium. The American contact person is Mark Seem, 450 Waverly Avenue, Brooklyn, N.Y. 11238, U.S.A., or Sheila Koren and Don Obers, c/o *State and Mind.* See IX-c, The European Network for Alternatives to Psychiatry.

Arbours Housing Association, Ltd. 55 Dartmouth Park Road, London NW5, England.

Another group that emerged from Kingsley Hall; set up by Burke and Schatzman. They have a more structured approach than the Philadelphia Association. They operate a crisis centre and several long term communities in London, and also publish a newsletter.

COPE. Office & Basement, 11 Acklam Road, London W10, England.

Mental patients self-help group, active in several areas including workshops, encounter groups, a day drop-in centre, Gay COPE, and publishing anti-psychiatry literature. They have recently opened a crisis centre at 49 Portnall Road, London W9.

EPOC Collective. c/o 111 Tavistock Crescent, London W11, England.

Publishing collective loosely connected with COPE. They produce *Heavy Daze.*

Mental Patients Union (MPU). National Information Centre, c/o Hull MPU, 16 Clifton Gardens, St. Georges Road, Hull HU3 3QB, England.

A federation of mental patients groups active in England, Wales, and Scotland. Based on the ideas that mental patients organize and support each other and fight for each other's rights.

East London MPU. 37 Mayola Road, London E5, England.

Philadelphia Association. 74a Portland Road, London W11, England.

Founded by Laing, Cooper, Esterson and others. They have several self-governing households for ex-psychiatric inmates. Kingsley Hall was one of their early projects. See II-a, British Anti-Psychiatry and X-a, Classic Experiments in Anti-Psychiatry.

PNP — People Not Psychiatry/People Need People. c/o Kevin Leather, 1 Bessbrook Rd., Liverpool L17, England, and c/o Chris, 49 Ravenhurst Rd., Harbourne, Birmingham E17, England.

The original alternative to psychiatry that started in the late 1960's. *PNP* is a network of people through which others can make contact and friends. There are several *PNP* groups in different parts of the country.

Radical Psychiatry Society. c/o 2 Primrose St., Lancaster, England.

Cahiers pour la Folie. c/o Mme. Hubert, 68 Rue d'Assas, Paris 75006, France.

Gardes-Fous. c/o Dr. Bernard de Freminville, 1 Rue des Fosses Saint-Jacques, Paris 75005, France.

GIA (Groupe Information Asile). 73 Rue Buffon, Paris 75005, France.

Psychiatrises en lutte. B.P. N° 60' — 75721 Paris Cedex 15, France.

GIA (Groupe Information Asile) — Belgium. c/o Yves-Luc Conreur, Rue Langeveld 146, 1180 Brussels, Belgium.

de Gekkenkrant. P.O. Box 3286, Amsterdam, the Netherlands. See XI-e, Periodicals.

Campaign Against Psychiatric Atrocities. c/o R. Povall, Box 6899, Auckland, New Zealand.

Research, legal, and publicity group.

Foundation for the Abolition of Compulsory Treatment. P.O. Box 3, Subiaco, West Australia.

Japanese Anti-Psychiatry Movement. Contact person: Toshiyuki Kusaka, Higashiyama 69-4, Nakahara-cho, Toyohashi-shi, Aichi-ken, Japan.

Kusaka is a Japanese activist resource person. He is active in a Toyohashi group and knows a lot about the Japanese movement.

b) Women's Groups

i) Canada

Feminist Therapist Listing — Vancouver Area. c/o Vancouver Status of Women, 1090 West 7th Avenue, Vancouver, B.C. V6H 1B3, Canada.

A periodically updated referral guide to feminist therapy available in Vancouver area. Includes the spectrum from feminist shrinks to gestalt, co-counselling, and group therapy.

Toronto Women's Counselling Collective. 15 Birch Street, Toronto, Ont. Canada.

ii) United States

Alternatives for Women. 40 East 14th Street, Tucson, Az., U.S.A.

Feminist counselling and therapy referral group.

Alyssum: A Center for Feminist Consciousness. 1719 Union Street, San Francisco, Ca. 94123, U.S.A.

Feminist therapy with emphasis on spirituality. This center is where Mander and Rush work. Also see their writings in VII-d, Feminist Therapy and VII-e, Feminist Spirituality.

Center for Feminist Therapy. (415) 398-8207, San Francisco, Ca., U.S.A.

Cleveland Women's Counselling. P.O. Box 18472, Cleveland, Oh. 44118, U.S.A.

Counselling Resource Center for Lesbians, 3532 North Halsted, Chicago, Ill. 60657, U.S.A.

Elizabeth Stone House. 108 Broadside Avenue, Jamaica Plain, Ma. 02130, U.S.A.

Pioneer feminist therapeutic community and crisis center for women. State funded. Also see articles about it in VII-d, Feminist Therapy.

Feminist Center for Human Growth & Development, Inc. 40 East 68th Street, New York, N.Y. 10021, U.S.A.

Non-profit educational corporation; offers lectures, panels, and interactive and participatory experimental workshops. It is committed to combatting sexism.

Feminist Therapy Referral Collective. 749 West End Avenue, Apt. 1W, New York, N.Y. 10025, U.S.A.

Growing Women. 121 - 12th Street S.E., Apt. 401, Washington, D.C. 20003, U S.A.

A collective that is putting together a women's therapeutic community and crisis residence. They now have a country farmhouse near Washington D.C. This project will be a women's farm operating on feminist principles. They welcome any donations of money, furniture, farm equipment, skills, and energy.

KNOW, Inc. P.O. Box 86031, Pittsburgh, Pa. 15221, U.S.A.

Distributes information packets, reprints of articles, etc. dealing with women and psychiatry/psychology plus other feminist topics.

Los Angeles Radical Feminist Therapy Collective. c/o The Women's Center, 237 Hill Street, Santa Monica, Ca., U.S.A.

A group of "non-certified, anti-professional radical feminists" using radical therapy for feminist political action.

National Feminist Therapist Association. N.F.T.A. Committee, Carolyn Mills Kroes, 11579 - 168th Avenue, Grant Haven, Mi. 49417, U.S.A.

Being formed by therapists and people interested in therapy who are concerned about eradicating sexist values and attitudes in current practice. This group is also anxious to block the legislative push in Maine and Michigan to limit the practice of psychotherapy to Ph.D.'s.

New York Feminist Therapist Referral Service. 312 West 82nd Street, New York, N.Y. 10024, U S.A.

Mental Health Task Force. California N.O.W., c/o Ollie Mae Bozarth, 2277 Fulton, No. 203, San Francisco, Ca. 94117, U.S.A.

Task force on mental health established by the National Organization for Women. It is dedicated to combatting forced psychiatric procedures, investigating alternatives, and educating professionals about the particular vulnerability of women due to sex-role stereotyping. People interested in starting a local task force, or in supporting the national work should write to this address.

Philadelphia Feminist Therapy Collective. 2131 Lombard Street, Philadelphia, Pa. 19146, U.S.A.

Individual and group feminist therapy by a collective of women trained as psychologists and social workers.

Support for Women in Madness (S.W.I.M.). c/o Las Hermanas, 4003 Wabash, San Diego, Ca. 92104, U.S.A.

Women Against Electric Shock Treatment. 5251 Broadway, Oakland, Ca. 94618, U.S.A.

Information exchange collective. Also see VII-c, Women: Self-Help.

Women Against Psychiatric Assault (WAPA). 558 Capp Street, San Francisco, Ca. 94110, U.S.A.

Anti-psychiatry group affiliated with Network Against Psychiatric Assault.

Women Against Psychiatric Assault – Denver. c/o Woman to Woman Bookstore, 2023 Colfax Avenue, Denver, Co. 80206, U.S.A

Women Against Psychiatric Assault – Los Angeles. P.O. Box 3921, Hollywood Station, Ca. 90028, U.S.A.

Women's Counselling and Resource Center. 1555 Massachusetts Avenue, Cambridge, Ma. 02138, U.S.A.

Women's Counselling Center. Lesbian Alliance, Box 11983, Wellston Station, St. Louis, Mo. 63112, U.S.A.

Women's Counselling Project. Room 112, Earl Hall, Columbia University, 117th Street and Broadway, New York, N.Y. 10027, U.S.A.

Women's Counselling Service. 2000 South 5th Street, Minneapolis, Mn. 55404, U.S.A.

Women's Crisis Center. c/o St. Andrews Church, 306 North Division, Ann Arbor, Mi. 48104, U S.A.

Women's Mental Health Project. 1915 N.E. Everett, Portland, Or. 97232, U.S.A.

Women's Psychotherapy Referral Service. c/o Dr. Susan Schad-Summers, 43 Fifth Avenue, New York, N.Y. 10003, U.S.A.

Women's Therapy Referral Service. P.O. Box 186, Southport, Ct. 06490, U.S.A.

iii) International

Women and Psychiatry. c/o South London Women's Liberation Centre, 14 Radnor Terrace, London SW8, England.

A group of women working on the rights of women and their treatment within the NHS psychiatric services.

c) Other Groups

Bay Area Bisexual Center. 1209 Sutter Street, Apt. 1643, San Francisco, Ca. 94109, U.S.A.

Recently opened "to provide a base of strength and sense of community for people who do or wish to relate to both women and men". Publishes bi-monthly newsletter.

Benjamin Rush Society. c/o Francis Touchet, 345 West 88th Street, New York, N.Y. 10024, U.S.A.

An organization devoted to studying the behavioral sciences from a Marxist viewpoint. They hold meetings and workshops and publish a newsletter.

The Body Politic. Box 7289, Stn. A, Toronto, Ont. M5W 1X9, Canada.

Has good listings of various gay and lesbian groups across Canada. See XI-e, Periodicals.

Children's Rights Workshop. 73 Balfour Square, London SE17, England.

Concerned with the rights of children. Good information source for alternative education, free schools, etc.

Coalition to Stop Institutional Violence. P.O. Box 1, Cambridge, Ma. 02139, U.S.A.

Fat Underground. 1102 - 1104 West Washington Blvd., Venice, Ca. 90291, U.S.A.

Fat militant collective dedicated to smashing oppression and exploitation of fat people.

Mohawks and Squaws. c/o The Jewish Community Center, 50 Sutherland Street, Brighton, Ma., U.S.A.

An activist group for mentally retarded adults working to change their status.

National Committee to Support the Marion Brothers. 6199 Waterman, St. Louis, Mo. 63112, U.S.A.

Support group for control unit prisoners at Marion Federal prison.

National Prison Project. c/o ACLU, 1346 Connecticut Ave. N.W., Suite 1031, Washington, D.C. 20036, U.S.A.

This group is doing work on prisoners' rights issues, including the forced drugging of prisoners.

Youth Liberation. 2007 Washtenaw Avenue, Ann Arbor, Mi. 48104, U.S.A.

Publishes news and educational materials about all aspects of youth liberation. See XI-c, Pamphlets and XI-e, Periodicals.

APPENDIX C: MAIN TRENDS IN ANTI-PSYCHIATRY — A SIMPLIFIED QUASI-DOGMATIC CHART

SCHOOL	SOURCES	PREMISES	PROGRAM
British Anti-Psychiatry			
Arbours Association Philadelphia Association Mary Barnes Joseph Berke David Cooper Aaron Esterson R.D. Laing Morton Schatzman Basic Document: R. D. Laing's **The Politics of Experience and the Bird of Paradise.**	Conventional training in medicine and psychiatry. Psychoanalysis. European Existential philosophers. Sartre's Dialectical Critique. Phenomenology. Sociological studies in "mental illness" (Goffman, Bateson, etc.). Studies in altered states of consciousness. New Left of the 1960's.	Our social structure is inherently oppressive: it perpetuates violence and mystifies experience: being in an untenable position can produce madness. The family plays a particularly oppressive role. People get contradictory linguistic messages: they create personal responses to these that are considered mad. The behavior of "schizophrenics" is intelligible when examined in its social context.	More flexible alternatives to the present family and social structures. Free up personal relationships. Use madness as a healing tool: it can be breakthrough, liberation, and renewal. Psychotherapy as a relationship between two people rediscovering their wholeness. Psychotherapy could include re-enactment of birth experience under guidance of psychiatric "midwife".
American Civil Liberties			
American Civil Liberties Union (ACLU) Associations for the Abolition of Involuntary Mental Hospitalization LAMP Center for the Study of Psychiatry Peter Breggin Thomas S. Szasz E. Fuller Torrey Basic Document: Thomas Szasz's **The Manufacture of Madness**	Conventional training in medicine, psychiatry and law. Historical works on psychiatric incarceration (Packard, Foucault, etc.). General history dealing with medicine, healing, deviance, and persecution. Records of litigation cases. Educational models of psychotherapy. Political philosophy of Libertarianism. The American Constitution.	"Mental illness" is a myth manufactured by our scientific/technological society. The medical model is inappropriate for problems of living. Mental patients are the scapegoats of an intolerant society. Current psychiatric practices are unconstitutional. Psychiatric confinement is often a response to a "housing problem" for the poor, elderly, incorrigible, etc.	Abolish the medical model; replace it with an educational one. Abolish all involuntary hospitalization and treatments. Ensure everyone's right to trial and due process. Raise the consciousness of doctors and lawyers. Neurologists should treat the few patients with proven organic brain disease. Psychotherapy as a voluntary contractual relationship between therapist and client.

SCHOOL	SOURCES	PREMISES	PROGRAM
Radical Psychiatry			
Bay Area Radical Therapy Collective Issues in Radical Therapy (IRT) Collective Claude Steiner Hogie Wyckoff Basic Document: IRT's **Readings in Radical Psychiatry**	Conventional training in psychology. Transactional Analysis (Eric Berne). Writings of Movement Groups (Blacks, Radical Feminists, Gays, Fat Liberation, etc.).	Oppression is internalized, thus leading to oppressive "games" and "life scripts". The psychiatric profession monopolizes the role of "mental healer" in order to pacify the oppressed, and for financial gain. Psychiatric deception compounds the alienation of mental patients. OPPRESSION + DECEPTION = ALIENATION. Paranoia is a state of heightened awareness and sensitivity to a true state of oppression. OPPRESSION + AWARENESS = ANGER.	Abolish the psychiatric profession's monopoly, and curtail its power. Return the art of soul-healing to its non-medical origins. Therapy in groups can combat internalized oppression. Transactional analysis as a tool for learning healthier scripts. "Radical psychiatry as a form of grassroots organizing." AWARENESS + CONTACT = LIBERATION.
Marxist Psychology			
Heidelberg Socialist Patients Collective (S.P.K.) Phil Brown Gracie Lyons Basic Document: Phil Brown's **Toward a Marxist Psychology**	Conventional training in psychology. Writings of Marx, Engels, and Mao Tse-Tung. Mainstream anti-psychiatry writers (Laing, Szasz, etc.) Writings of movement groups (Mental Patients Liberation, Blacks, Gays, Radical Feminists, etc.)	The capitalist system forces internalization of problems, and a false consciousness: thus the worker is alienated from self, work, and others. Many problems of living are not individual, but are common to all persons in a social class. The pseudo-science of psychology, while overtly liberal, keeps the oppressed adjusted to their oppression. Mental institutions are storage places for non-cooperative workers.	Socialist revolution to externalize problems: to find the social reasons, and collective answers, to them. Develop a "people's psychology" that allows the masses to transform their lives through self-directed activity. Practice criticism/self-criticism to resolve contradictions inside the individual and within/among groups.

School	Sources	Premises	Program
Mental Patients Liberation			
North American Conference on Human Rights & Psychiatric Oppression Ex-psychiatric Inmates Groups (MPA, NAPA, COPE, etc.) EPOC Collective Madness Network News State & Mind (RT) Collective Basic Document: **Position Paper of the Fourth Annual North American Conference on Human Rights and Psychiatric Oppression**	Testimonies of psychiatric inmates and ex-inmates. Studies and documents of psychiatric abuse. Mainstream anti-psychiatry writers (Laing, Szasz, etc.) Socialist theory. Writings of other movement groups (Prisoners, Gays, Blacks, Radical Feminists, etc.)	"Mentalism" is the force that discredits non-sanctioned conduct and experience by labelling them symptoms of mental illness. Psychiatry serves as one of the ruling class' tools for general social control. The mental illness system "blames the victim", teaching us that our problems are signs of personal weakness, not the result of social conditions; thus we cannot fight back collectively.	Abolish the mental illness system. Eliminate all forms of oppression: mentalism, sexism, racism, ageism, capitalism, etc. Mental patients organizing against psychiatric abuse, from grass-roots to international levels. An analysis of psychiatric oppression by patients and ex-patients, not professionals. Create alternatives to psychiatry, such as small voluntary support groups (asking for help is a normal human need; giving help a normal human role.)
Feminist Therapy			
Feminist Therapy Collectives Phyllis Chesler Sara David Anica Vesel Mander Anne Kent Rush Elizabeth Friar Williams Basic Document: Phyllis Chesler's **Women and Madness**	Conventional training in psychiatry, psychology, and sociology. Insights and techniques from some of the so-called "hip therapies" (Gestalt, Bodywork, Assertiveness Training, etc.) Writings of mainstream feminist theorists (Millett, Firestone, etc.) The emerging academic field of Women's Studies.	The rigidly defined passive, subservient roles for women in patriarchal society lead to feelings of powerlessness and depression, particularly during middle age. Both the polarization of sex roles and the mind/body split fostered by society are sources of alienation. What psychiatrists call "mental health" is often the measure of people's adjustment to their sex role stereotype.	Rid psychiatry of its sexist beliefs and practices. Women gaining equal power in the world. Transform people into more androgynous beings. Work towards a more co-operative, collective society. Self-help and self-defence skills for women and other oppressed groups. Rediscover male-suppressed women's culture as a valuable source of strength.

THE WOODCUTS

The illustrations in this book are prints made from woodcuts designed and carved by the author. The anti-psychiatry movement, like other ideological forces, has been developing a body of visual images which adds a dimension to its political analysis. In these illustrations, the author has freely borrowed from these existing images—copying, modifying, expanding—as well as adding new material from her own experiences and perceptions.

The initial inspiration for these prints came from Hieronymus Bosch's 15th century painting *The Cure of Folly* (which was loosely copied for the woodcut VI *Professionalism and the Mental Health Industry*). In this painting, Bosch made an attack on the quackery of his time. The scene depicts a "Medicine Master" with a funnel on his head (a symbol of the charlatan) attempting to cure his patient by cutting the stone of folly out of his skull. The others in the scene willingly participate, having been duped by his quackery.

The woodcut V *Mind Control Technology* is a contemporary update of *The Cure of Folly.* The central circle image and the "Medicine Master" appearing in the upper left are copies of the powerful anti-psychosurgery graphics produced in 1973 by Seed/Liberation News Service.

Images appearing in the other wooducts come from varied sources. These include: anti-psychiatry demonstration photos from *Madness Network News,* pictures from *Mary Barnes: Two Accounts of a Journey Through Madness*, historical medical illustrations, medieval manuscript designs, contemporary drug ads, photos of women Karate black belts and painter Aubrey Dayman, an etching by William Blake, portraits derived from the author's sketching trips to skid row coffeeshops and Riverview Psychiatric Hospital, a logo from the Vancouver People's Law School, and other miscellaneous sources.

Hand-printed, signed copies of the eleven woodcuts are available for purchase in unlimited editions. Inquiries should be sent to Press Gang Publishers.

THE AUTHOR

K. Portland Frank is a lesbian/feminist, artist, and former mental patient. Her psychiatric incarceration took place in the mid-sixties during a time of emotional crisis while she was a student nurse at St. Mary's Hospital in Montreal; as a result, she was promptly kicked out of the nursing school and blacklisted from entering others. During the following half-decade or so she continued to seek "help" from a series of shrinks and also tried to redeem herself with the health establishment by studying psychology at Simon Fraser University. While a student at SFU she avidly devoured all the books and articles on "mental illness" she could get her hands on and, eventually, began reading the works of Laing, Szasz, the radical feminists, *The Radical Therapist,* etc. In 1972 she completed her B.A., discovered the Vancouver Mental Patients Association, and went on to spend most of the next 4 years living in M.P.A. group homes. It was during this time that she began compiling *The Anti-Psychiatry Bibliography*, broke her long-standing addiction to the mental health system, and made a commitment to doing artwork as a lifetime career. She also studied at the Vancouver School of Art, from which she graduated in 1978. Her work has appeared in *Madness Unmasked, Mental Patients and the Law* (Vancouver People's Law School Handbook), *In A Nutshell, Makara, Kinesis, The Kite,* and the *Press Gang Calendar.* At present, she is working on a forthcoming book of annotated woodcuts about women, to be called *The Book of Amazons.*

Press Gang is a feminist publishing and printing collective. Since 1974, we have been producing books and other printed materials that provide an analytical view of the women's and anti-capitalist movements. *The Anti-Psychiatry Bibliography and Resource Guide* is our second book examining the oppression of people by the psychiatric establishment: *Women Look at Psychiatry*, published in 1976, is a collection of essays and personal accounts by women involved with psychiatry — as patients, professionals, or both.

Other books from Press Gang are:

Women Look at Psychiatry	Dorothy Smith and Sara David, eds.
An Account to Settle	Jackie Ainsworth et al.
Jody Said	Beth Jankola
Fishmarket and Other Poems	Phyllis Baker
Muktu: The Backward Muskox	Heather Kellerhals-Stewart and Karen Muntean, illustrator.